OXFORD MEDICAL PUBLICATIONS

Depression

THE FACTS

DEPRESSION

THE FACTS

By

GEORGE WINOKUR, MD
Department of Psychiatry
University of Iowa College of Medicine

OXFORD
OXFORD UNIVERSITY PRESS
NEW YORK TORONTO MELBOURNE
1981

Oxford University Press, Walton Street, Oxford OX2 6DP

London Glasgow New York Toronto
Delhi Bombay Calcutta Madras Karachi
Kuala Lumpur Singapore Hong Kong Tokyo
Nairobi Dar es Salaam Cape Town
Melbourne Wellington
and associate companies in
Beirut Berlin Ibadan Mexico City

British Library Cataloguing in Publication Data

Winokur, George
Depression. – (Oxford medical publications)
1. Depression, Mental
I. Title
616.89'5 RC537
ISBN 0-19-261315-4

Set by Hope Services, Abingdon
Printed in Great Britain by
Richard Clay (The Chaucer Press) Ltd,
Bungay, Suffolk

Preface

I went to medical school for two reasons, first because my parents told me to, and second because I was very impressed with Errol Flynn who played a bacteriologist in a movie, *Green Light*. As I recall the movie, Errol Flynn was on the verge of making an enormous contribution to humanity and I thought it would be nice to do the same. So in a sense perhaps this book ought to be dedicated to Errol Flynn, but, as he is better known for other kinds of things than his role in *Green Light*, that doesn't seem appropriate. Anyway, after I entered medical school, I found myself interested in four things. I liked dermatology because I was fascinated with the scroungy, low life diseases which were seen in that clinic. I liked obstetrics because I enjoyed the excitement that almost invariably occurred at the time of birth and the enormous good feelings that existed after a normal baby was delivered. Most of all I was interested in research and in psychiatry. In the summer of 1946 with the help of a faculty member in the medical school, I did research that was pertinent to the immunology of cancer. A fellow medical student and I were rather convinced at that time that immunology might provide some of the answers to cancer. We found that human serum agglutinated mouse red blood cells and coined the term the 'MO agglutinin'. It was in the heyday of the discovery of the Rh factor that we published a paper. We were sorry to learn that we had been beaten to the 'MO' finding by another investigator some time before. I was equally interested in psychiatry. I found the subject-matter fascinating but mostly I thought that if I knew more about psychiatry, I would really know what made people tick, really understand what went on in their minds. I would really understand their motivation and why they did things. At this point, I might say that I did go into psychiatry and I do not believe I understand the mind any better than I did before going into psychiatry. What's more I do not believe that my colleagues in psychiatry, no matter what they say, really understand motivation or what makes a person behave or think as he does. Many of them say they do but I do not believe them.

Upon graduation from medical school, I had one of two choices, to go into immunology research or to go into psychiatry. I talked to a very wise travelling salesman in Baltimore who pointed out to me that I was perfectly well trained to be a clinical psychiatrist but that I should have a Ph.D. to go into immunology. That seemed eminently reasonable, so I decided to enter a psychiatric residency. For a number of years, I was mainly interested in a psychosocial viewpoint about psychiatric illness and psychiatric syndromes. In the early 1960s a colleague and I engaged in a study to test whether early bereavement or loss of parent was relevant to depression in later life. Inadvertently we appended a systematic family history to our investigation. We found that early bereavement or separation was irrelevant to the development of depression but we found that psychiatric illnesses were found in families of psychiatric patients more frequently than one would expect by chance. Also, the same psychiatric illnesses seemed to run in families. Thus, I became interested in family studies and genetics and once having made this turn I decided that psychiatric illnesses and particularly the mood illnesses (depressions and manias) were best studied under the imprimatur of the medical model. It seemed that most psychiatric illnesses had a familial and probably genetic basis; at least this was true of most serious psychiatric illnesses. This was certainly so in the mood illnesses. This meant that there was some kind of underlying biological background. Also, these illnesses could be defined in the same way as any ordinary medical illness could be defined.

In the early 1960s, the Chairman of the Department of Psychiatry in which I functioned was Dr Eli Robins. It was he, in fact, who stimulated my inclinations in the direction of the medical model. Interestingly, we never discussed it as the medical model. Robins simply talked about it in terms of the fact that we were doctors and should function as doctors. So we now have five people to whom I owe a debt of gratitude, namely my parents, Errol Flynn, a travelling salesman, and Eli Robins. To this group I would like to add my wife, who is a social worker. I owe her a debt of gratitude for not having bugged me about my lack of psychosocial orientation. On occasion, she had to defend my viewpoint among her more psychologically oriented friends. She did this well.

This book recognizes that there is a large body of data about the mood disorders. If anything, that body of data is the largest of all of the psychiatric illnesses. Of course, there seems to be plenty of room for opinion, and I have certainly attempted to make that clear in the text. A large number of people suffer from mood disorders. They are not usually impecunious. They are usually solid citizens often wealthy and occasionally distinguished. They make up a very large part of the psychiatrist's practice. Often in their milder forms, mood disorders are seen by non-physicians or by general practitioners. In any event, it behoves the person who has a mood disorder to know about the illness, much in the same way that it behoves a diabetic to know about his illness. It is also useful for the family to know about the illness. It is equally as important for family practitioners, hospital doctors, other doctors, psychologists, social workers, and other professionals to know about the illness. They may or may not be particularly involved in dealing with depressed and manic patients, but it is important that they have some concept of this in order that they might appropriately obtain help for them. This then is the reason for the book.

I think I need to make a few more acknowledgements. I would like to thank my secretary Joyce Sweeting, for her untiring work in getting the manuscript out. Likewise, I would like to thank Jeaneen Field, who also made a large contribution to the preparation. Patricia Winokur made an important contribution to simplifying the language; I hope enough.

Finally, I would like to thank the members of the Department of Psychiatry of the University of Iowa College of

Medicine because without their stimulating interaction I do not think I would be motivated to do very much.

Iowa
December 1980 GW

Contents

1

Darkness over Yasnaya Polyana

'Clear Glade': that is the meaning of Yasnaya Polyana. It was the ancestral estate of Leo Tolstoy. In ordinary times it was a happy place, but as Tolstoy neared his fiftieth year it became the stage on which Tolstoy's depression was played out.

For Tolstoy it was the period during which he was finishing *Anna Karenina.* According to his son, Ilya, Tolstoy felt that only death lay in the immediate future. Enthusiasms were hard to rekindle. He had the fantasy of hanging over a deep pit, clinging to a root which was being severed by two mice. Below him was horror.

Because of this despair, his entire family suffered. His son remembers this period – the period of his own adolescence – as gloomy and unpromising, in contrast to his sunny childhood. Tolstoy himself was morose and irritable which was unlike his usual self. His relations with his wife deteriorated and he continually castigated her and threatened separation.

Of this time Tolstoy wrote in his confession:

> The thought of suicide came to me as naturally as thoughts about improving life had come to me formerly. This thought was so tempting that I had to use guile against myself so as not to bring it to fulfilment too hastily . . . I . . . used to hide a rope lest I should hang myself on the cross beam of the bookshelves in the room where I undressed alone every night, and gave up hunting with a gun lest I should be tempted by so easy a way of delivering myself from life.

Such a depression as Tolstoy experienced is not really unusual. In fact, it is so common that almost everybody has some experience of this phenomenon, either personally, or through their family and friends.

What is especially unusual about depression is that the borderline between unhappiness and a disease is blurred. Many of the symptoms of depression are simply a natural response to tragic events in people's lives. For instance, sadness and preoccupation with a dark future are not uncommon after the death of somebody close. But, depression is also a disease. The difference is that on the one hand depression which is a response to an unfortunate event is perceived as a natural part of life by a person who experiences it. On the other hand, a person suffering from depression as a disease or an illness feels a sense of discontinuity, a change from his usual self. The person believes himself to be in some sense different. He is likely to believe that he is losing his mind. These are uncommon feelings when a person is simply responding to a disturbing event in his life.

Tolstoy's son believed that his father was undergoing some kind of spiritual change, that he was responding to disillusionment, and that he was groping for a rebirth of interest. However, certainly, there was no obvious unhappy life event that occurred before Tolstoy's depression. He was a successful author at that time, highly regarded and famous, and there were no unusual financial stresses. Thus, it is equally possible that his state of mind was a simple manifestation of an illness.

This is the point of departure for this book. The fact of the matter is that it is quite possible to describe depression systematically as an illness, to discuss causative factors, to describe a clinical picture, to follow the course of the illness, and to prescribe appropriate treatment. Exciting progress has been made in depression, and it is even possible to discuss relevant laboratory tests. Depressive illness may be dealt with as any other medical entity and we propose to approach it in this fashion.

2

The definition and clinical appearance of depression

Depression is ubiquitous but so also is unhappiness. They are not the same, but because they occur so frequently they are considered identical by many people, even professionals. Unhappiness occurs in the lives of all people. The college student who fails an examination responds to this kind of life stress by feeling defeated and often morose. These feelings and this mood last only a short time, perhaps a few days to a week. The student usually then puts in a great amount of effort and brings his marks up to a passing level or better. The coal-miner who is laid off work or who is involved in a long strike is unhappy for as long as he is out of work. After all, he has difficulty in providing for his family and feels somewhat diminished by the fact that he is not involved in his usual role in life. At no point is either the college student or the coal-miner incapacitated. In both cases they function well, and with an improvement in circumstances they brighten up and appear quite normal. What they are showing is simply a response to a difficult situation in their lives. This is not to be considered a depression. There is no way to protect human beings from vicissitudes of this kind. Some life stresses are important and some are trivial. Generally, they are not controllable; and it is natural that a person will respond to them with unhappiness.

Depression, on the other hand, is a clinical state often requiring intervention. It may be defined as a state of mind and body which is characterized by a change in mood towards being miserable, worried, discouraged, irritable, unable to feel emotion, fearful, despondent, hopeless, or down in the dumps. This state of mind, however, is not enough for the diagnosis of depression. In addition, the depressed person must have a cluster of associated symptoms which occur over a period of time and are associated with the mood. Such symptoms are a poor appetite or weight loss, trouble sleeping, tiredness or fatiguability, agitation, slowness in thinking or motion, a loss of interest in usual activities, a decrease in sexual drive, feelings of self-condemnation, difficulty in thinking or concentrating, thoughts of death or suicide, and suicide attempts. Of course, not all of these symptoms will be present in each person, but several should be reported in order to make a diagnosis of depression. Also, there is a time factor. It would be unlikely that the person who suffered from these symptoms over a three-day period would be considered as having a depression, though this is not absolutely impossible. On the other hand, an individual who has such a cluster of symptoms, who considers this clinical state to be different from his usual self, and who suffers from the symptoms for over a month would undoubtedly be considered as showing a clinical depression. The question of severity also has to be taken into account, and this can be assessed by determining whether or not the person is able to function in the community and perform his usual tasks. The need for help, or intervention, or hospitalization indicates a kind of continuum of severity. No doubt there are people who suffer from the sort of depression described above who never receive any help and who weather the circumstances on their own. These people also should be clearly recognized as depressed.

The appearance of a depressed patient is often very striking. At home or on the ward of a hospital, he may be extremely agitated, wringing his hands, twisting a handkerchief, rubbing his head, or pacing back and forth. Or he may sit in a bland, dull way on the periphery of group, only interacting or responding to other people in a slow and monotonous fashion. His brow may be furrowed. Often his eyes will be glassy and red. He is on the periphery of the group not because he has been excluded, but rather because he has little to say and finds no pleasure in socialization. His response to a question will take a long time in coming. An examiner will find it painful to wait for the response. The patient may have lost weight, and his skin may hang in folds. He may moan and describe himself as a great sinner. Often he will believe that his very existence bodes ill for his family. His future is perceived as grim, and only death may be considered a reasonable way out of his dilemma. He may lie in bed and be immovable. He will not try to accomplish simple tasks and will say that it would be useless to do so because of his worthlessness. Perhaps one of the most important things about the depressed person is that though he appears dull he is clearly in considerable pain. He is not bland or flat, rather he is suffering. When such a person is brought into a discussion, he may at times begin to talk quite rapidly, but shortly after this he will revert to slowness and uninterest. The symptoms that have been described above may seem worse in the morning and improve over the day, or there may be no change with time of day. What is most important is that the patient presents himself in the blackest of moods and he can see no possibility that any lightening can occur. After all, how could so great a sinner expect anything better?

This is the picture of an individual who is severely depressed. Few people would have any difficulty recognizing such a state. However, it should be noted that though the symptoms may be similar, many patients are far less socially incapacitated; indeed in some cases the symptoms are present, but they are subtle and require some background and experience to recognize. Often the depressive syndrome may manifest itself only by a change in the person's feelings about himself, some lack of energy, and a feeling of melancholy. These mild symptoms might last weeks or months and be relatively unresponsive to environmental circumstances.

Table 2.1 shows the frequency of symptoms in a group of depressive patients who were hospitalized.

Some of the symptoms speak for themselves but others require some discussion. 'Anorexia' is defined as a lack of appetite; it is often associated with loss of weight. However, loss of appetite is more common than weight loss, so that the physical evidence of loss of appetite is not always present.

Table 2.1

Symptoms occurring in hospitalized depressed patients

Symptoms	Patients showing symptoms (%)
Reduced energy level	97
Impaired concentration	84
Anorexia	80
Initial insomnia	77
Loss of interest	77
Difficulty starting activities	76
Worrying more than usual	69
Subjective agitation	67
Slowed thinking	67
Difficulty with decision-making	67
Terminal insomnia	65
Suicide ideation or plans	63
Weight loss	61
Tearfulness	61
Movements slowed (subjective perception)	60
Increased irritability	60
Feels will never get well	56

Symptoms were considered present if they represented a change from level of functioning. (From Baker *et al. Comprehensive Psychiatry* (1971).)

'Loss of interest' is a very important symptom. It manifests itself by the individual's finding that he gets little pleasure in usual activities, and therefore he does not involve himself in them as much as he did before. Consequently one may note for instance, that the depressed person no longer attends church as frequently as he did before. He may be less interested in going to the cinema or watching television. He may have no interest in reading the daily newspaper. 'Subjective agitation' is present when the patient describes himself as feeling agitated or shaky inside. It is not necessary that such agitation be manifest on observation; rather it is a complaint instead of a sign of the illness. 'Slow thinking' is also called 'retardation'. The person believes that his usual rapid way of grasping things is impaired and that he is unable to handle ordinary amounts of information because of the slowness of his thinking processes. Often the depressed person has trouble making a decision. One of the most common symptoms in depression is that of difficulty in sleeping, and this manifests itself in two ways. Sometimes the person has trouble getting to sleep. This is a symptom which depressives share with patients who have other psychiatric diagnoses. A more reliable symptom of depression is that of 'terminal insomnia' or waking up in the early part of the morning and being unable to get back to sleep. This is probably as typical a symptom of depression as can be found. 'Tearfulness' is easily defined, but one of the things that should be recognized is that certain depressed patients, particularly those who are seen in later life, often complain of the inability to cry, even though they feel tearful. Finally, the patient who 'feels he will never get well' is manifesting a kind of hopelessness.

Special symptoms of depression

There are a number of symptoms which are seen in depression but which do not occur in half of the cases. Nevertheless they are not rare and they are often of considerable importance. One of these is 'diurnal variation'. The typical diurnal variation in a depressed person may be described as a change in mood state as the day wears on. Thus, the person will get up in the morning feeling very depressed, hopeless, and showing considerable slowness in his movements and thinking (retardation). As the day wears on he feels more normal and by night time the person feels almost, though not necessarily quite, normal. A good example of this is one patient who was seen clinically over several months for depression. She had all of the ordinary symptoms of depression and also showed considerable diurnal variation. In the morning when she woke, she was grossly suicidal and, in fact, made several suicide attempts. (One of these attempts was serious: she attempted to hang herself with a tie she was knitting for the psychiatrist. As luck would have it, the tie broke and the patient lived, though she had a serious rope burn on her neck for some time.) By mid-afternoon she had improved, and by suppertime she was close to, though not quite, normal. This occurred day after day. When seen by the doctor in the morning, she showed marked suicidal trends. When seen in the late afternoon, these had all dissipated. She never developed any insight into this pattern. Thus, for a period of several months she continued to change diurnally. She never learned that her self-condemnation was inappropriate and only occurred in the morning and therefore was not to be acted upon.

Many patients with depression show a decreased interest in sexual behaviour. It is not that such patients have an inability to perform the sexual act, but rather that their interest has decreased to such an extent that they make no effort to engage in sexual activity.

About a third of the patients suffer from anxiety attacks. These occur only with the onset of the depression and during the depression and disappear when the depression has terminated. An anxiety attack manifests itself by a feeling of impending doom and a series of associated symptoms such as complaints of palpitations of the heart, dizziness, sweating and shortness of breath, and chest pain. There is an illness called 'anxiety neurosis' which is chronic and which shows such symptoms over a period of many, many years. The anxiety attacks associated with depression unlike those of anxiety neurosis are not chronic and are limited to the period of depression.

Often depressed patients complain of vague physical symptoms, such as back pain, or joint pain, or abdominal pain. Relatively few patients complain of burning pains in their body, but these may be of special significance. One patient who was seen on a consultation service complained of burning pain in his feet after having had frostbite. He was an elderly man and he denied a depressive mood. Also, he did not show very many of the associated symptoms that one frequently sees in depression. Nevertheless, upon discharge from the hospital, he went home and committed suicide. In retrospect, it would appear that more attention should have been paid to the significance of a constant, burning pain. Vague complaints of difficulties in the chest or in the head are not infrequent in depression.

Ruminations of guilt are seen in about a third of the patients. Often the patient will think back over the years and centre on one circumstance. One man who was admitted for a depression in his middle fifties recalled that thirty years prior to admission he had cheated the government out of a small amount of money on his income tax. Nothing had happened to him. For thirty years he had had no depression, but when he finally suffered from the illness, this small dishonesty became a mountainous problem for him. He constantly fretted about it. He felt terribly guilty and could think of nothing else for a long period of time. When he had improved, he recognized the absurdity of his behaviour.

Some patients develop 'delusions', that is fixed false ideas. Usually these have a depressive quality. Thus, a delusional person may believe that he is being spied on and persecuted by the government for something which he has done and for which he has every right to feel guilty. Nevertheless, the delusion is that he is being spied on at all. It is the guilt that gives the delusion its depressive quality. Sometimes one sees nihilistic delusions in depression. An example of this is the woman who believed that she did not have any intestines in her abdomen or another person who believed that part of his brain had rotted out.

Occasionally one finds delusions which do not have a depressive quality. Thus, sometimes delusions will occur which have nothing to do with guilt, or sinfulness, or worthlessness, or failure. An example of this would be somebody who believed that the furniture in the room had been altered to irritate him. Such non-depressive delusions are not common but they are seen.

About a quarter of the patients communicate suicidal ideas or plans or attempts, but only about 15 per cent of depressive patients who are admitted to the hospital have really made an attempt to take their own lives. Finally, note should be made of the fear of losing one's mind. This is not an uncommon symptom in depression. It shows the essential intactness of the depressive's thought processes. He realizes that he is not performing up to scratch and that he is not thinking as well as he has in the past. Consequently he believes that he is probably losing his mind and will soon be confined to a mental asylum. Nothing could be further from the truth, but there is no way to convince such a person of this. It is of considerable interest that patients who suffer from a bereavement (a death of a close relative or friend) may show the full panoply of depressive symptoms for some time. However, such grief-stricken patients do not ever believe that they are going to lose their minds. They recognize that their symptoms are a result of the bereavement. Thus, the symptom of being afraid of losing one's mind when observed has considerable importance, though it is not invariably found.

Along with a depressive mood and associated symptoms, certain kinds of behaviour occur. A few people suffering from depression will drink to excess even though this has never been part of their habitual behaviour. They will say that they drink in order to relieve the feelings of depression but whether this is to be accepted is questionable. In any case, as a result of their drinking, they may do certain things while inebriated for which they will be sorry in the future. As a consequence, some of the depressives who drink to excess during the episode of depression will become increasingly guilty because of their behaviour. Also, some depressives will become passive and accepting of things which ordinarily would have been anathema to them. A young woman who is depressed might conceivably get herself involved in a sexual liaison and become pregnant. Such cases have certainly been documented and pose considerable ethical problems when it comes to deciding whether such a pregnancy should be terminated. The problem is that such a pregnancy is a result of a woman's change in mood and behaviour.

Mania

Many depressives also suffer from 'manias'. On average about six to eight patients with depression are admitted to a psychiatric hospital for every one patient with a mania. In many patients, manias and depressions occur at different times in the life span. Thus, a person will be admitted for a mania on one occasion and for a depression on another occasion. Most depressives do not have manias at any time during their lives. There are probably about ten patients who never suffer a mania but do suffer depressions for every patient who suffers either manias only or manias and depressions. Whereas about 40 per cent of the patients who enter a psychiatric hospital have a mood disorder (manias and depression, manias only, or depressions only), only about a seventh or 6 per cent ever show a manic episode.

The person with an unequivocal mania is colourful and unforgettable. At the most extreme, he talks constantly. From his mouth comes a torrent of ideas and words. The ideas are related to each other but are so rapid that it is hard to follow his speech. Sometimes the manic patient will start with an idea and go on to a variety of other ideas only to come back to the original one. This is called circumstantiality. At other times, the manic makes jokes and puns and is generally great fun to hear. His attire may be unusual and often it is very bright. Colours clash. Socially, such a patient involves himself in everything. He is intrusive and irritates those about him. He is constantly attending to other people's business besides his own and this irritates his friends, his family, or even people who are attempting to deal with him in the hospital. For the manic patient, no circumstance is too large or too small on which to express an opinion. He may be constantly in motion as well as constantly talking. If he is prevented from carrying out some of these activities, he may become irritable and occasionally assaultive. He is grandiose and can accept no restraint on either his thinking or his activity. Often, he is supercilious and haughty. Sometimes he will be stimulated sexually. If he is at home, his wife may cry for help as a result of his excessive demands. Men who are married to manic women may complain of gross fatigue because their wives have kept them up all night with ever-increasing sexual provocation. The patient is filled with plans for making money and involves himself with money-making schemes, generally using very poor judgement. These are of the quality of planning for a summer resort on a barren island in the North Sea, with lavish facilities for water skiing. Not all manic patients are as severely affected as this. As in depression, the symptoms may be subtle and require some experience to recognize. A mild set of symptoms is referred to as a 'hypomania'. Like depression, however, the manic symptomatology is a clear change from the usual type of thought and behaviour that characterizes the individual.

Mania may be defined as a state of mind or body which manifests itself by a very elated mood (euphoria) or an irritable mood. The accompanying symptoms are racing thoughts, over-activity and overtalkativeness, distractibility, grandiosity, and a rush of speech. The symptoms of mania are presented in Table 2.2.

Table 2.2

The symptoms of mania

	Patients showing symptoms (%)
Euphoria	98
Irritability	85
Flight of ideas (racing thoughts)	93
Overtalkativeness	99
Distractibility	100
Grandiosity	86
Delusions	48
Financial extravagance	69
Fleeting episodes of depression	68
Sleep problems	90

(From G Winokur, P. Clayton, and T. Reich, *Manic depressive illness.* Mosby, St. Louis (1969).)

These symptoms are somewhat more unusual and uncommon than those of depression and, therefore, must be discussed in detail. 'Euphoria' refers to an elated mood. Some synonyms would be feeling on top of the world, tops, feeling better than ever, or some similar kind of statement. Usually 'irritability' accompanies euphoria but sometimes it is present by itself. In the expansive mood of the manic patient, any kind of restriction is met with irritability. The manic tends to be demanding because of this expansiveness and often finds himself frustrated in doing all of the things that he feels he would like to do. The cardinal symptoms are overactivity and 'overtalkativeness', and the complaint of 'racing thoughts' ('flight of ideas'). The manic patient states that his mind is running much faster than usual. 'Grandiosity' refers to the patient's feelings that he is omnipotent and can do anything. He may believe that he is unusually talented and should be recognized for this. Thus, he could conceivably run for a high office on the basis of a misconception about his own background. Financially, he tends to be very extravagant. He may spend a lot of money on things which he does not need. It is not uncommon for a manic patient to buy and sell several cars, losing money hand over fist. A manic physician who had many episodes used to speculate in the stock market during his manias and he did poorly. Also, he used to buy pairs of shoes and his cupboards were stuffed with unnecessary pairs that he bought at the time that he was manic.

Irritability without elation is seen only in a minority of cases. If the basic mood of the manic patient consists only of irritability, the clinical picture will appear somewhat different from that of those patients who are elated. Both irritable and elated manic patients, of course, show a flight of ideas. However, associated with elation there is frequently grandiosity and increased spending, a duet of symptoms which is not seen in the manic patient who displays only irritability.

Sleep is often decreased in mania. The person is so stimulated that he cannot find time to go to sleep; and, when he does lie down, his mind races so rapidly that sleep becomes impossible for him. At the same time he also often overeats. Unlike depressives who only infrequently abuse alcohol, manics are legendary in their ability to misuse alcohol. They are as extravagant with alcohol as they are with money.

If one allows a manic patient to talk, one will note that he shows fleeting episodes of depression embedded within the mania ('microdepressions'). He may be talking in a grandiose and extravagant fashion and then suddenly for thirty seconds breaks down to give an account of something he feels guilty about. For instance, he may be talking vigorously and in the midst of his loquacity he may suddenly talk about the death of his father for which he has felt guilty for some time. His eyes will fill with tears but in 15 to 30 seconds he will be back talking in his expansive fashion.

Often the manic episode will be preceded by a short episode of depression which will show the symptom picture of depression described earlier. After the manic episode is over, there will often be a depression lasting several months. The depressive episodes tend not to be acute or abrupt in formation, but rather occur over a period of some days or weeks or even months. A manic episode is much more likely to be abrupt.

Delusions and hallucinations are seen in mania. They are probably more common than in depression. Often they take a religious turn, and the patient may believe that he has been especially selected by God for certain kinds of purpose. Thus, many of the delusions are characterized by an elated mood and a feeling that one has a special purpose in life. Ideas of aristocratic descent, for example, believing oneself to be related to the Queen of England, are not uncommon. One manic man believed he was the reincarnation of Otto von Bismarck. Occasionally one encounters the manic who complains that he is controlled by some outside force or person (delusions of passivity).

Delusions and hallucinations are not all that uncommon in mania. However these delusions and hallucinations sometimes look atypical and suggest the idea that the person may be suffering from schizophrenia, a chronic disease characterized by bizarre thoughts. Delusions and hallucinations in mania tend to be relatively short-lived and of acute onset. They tend to be rather variable. For example, one patient's report stated 'recently she has been preoccupied with the thought of television and with the idea of her thought and speech being collected by radio, sorted out, and then transmitted throughout the state'. This was a patient whose diagnosis was unequivocally mania and who recovered. She had no other symptoms of schizophrenia. That same patient had a delusional perception in that she believed that her glasses were a sort of television, and she believed that her thoughts were being recorded. Another manic patient, a 20-year-old woman, 'began to talk about a message from her dead father, telling her to make the right hand do as much as the left and forced her husband into an elaborate ceremony in assisting with the housework'. A third manic woman of 26, 'felt that her home doctor hypnotized her and had a power over her so that he could impose strange things on her'. For instance, 'he made her skin itchy and made her want him'. She asked him to kiss her. These rather unusual delusions in the above three cases were associated with many other manic symptoms such as overtalkativeness, racing thoughts, and euphoria.

Grandiosity occurring even to a delusional extent was seen in a man who entered the hospital and believed that he was God. He spoke incessantly, had a flight of ideas, and felt omnipotent and extremely euphoric. After all, why shouldn't he, he was God. He would look out of the window and peruse the cloudy skies, say that when he felt bad the skies clouded up. When he was angry tornadoes and rain storms occurred; and since he was feeling rather well at that particular time, very shortly the sky would become a bright blue and the sun would shine. He came from a small town in Illinois, Kewanee, which he thought should be renamed 'New Bethlehem.'

Hypersexuality is a common symptom in mania. This symptom manifests itself by increased sexual contacts. A woman with five children who suffered from periodic manias would at these times constantly approach her husband for increased amounts of sexual intercourse, whereas during her states of being well she was very ordinary and, in fact, rather prim. During her manic episodes sex was constantly on her mind and she spent a great deal of time describing relationships with her husband in glowing and intimate terms. Specifically, what she was concerned with was whether or not they might be able to have their orgasms at exactly the same time during coitus. Promiscuity occasionally occurs and is probably more frequent in younger patients. Most patients who manifest hypersexuality do so in an acceptable fashion. There is a great deal of sexual display, often considerably more so than actual sexual acting out. A common sight is a man or woman who has a great flood of speech, is talking constantly, and is exposing himself or herself. The spouse or companion of the patient is often surprised at this behaviour and describes it as quite atypical of the individual when normal.

Finally, the symptom manifestations often lead to admission to hospital. In men the most common reasons for admission are extravagance, alcohol abuse, inability to work, the annoyance of family and friends at the patient's overtalkativeness, and overactivity. In women, the reasons for admission are somewhat different. They are sleeplessness, delusional or hallucinatory thinking, overtalkativeness, and overactivity, and, less commonly, extravagance and aggression or destructiveness. Women are rarely admitted because of alcohol abuse, sexual problems, or work disability.

Although women have traditionally had less control over their environment than men, it is interesting that the period of time from the onset of mania to hospitalization has been the same for many years in both sexes. Women have not been sent to hospital any earlier than men. Ordinarily the patient is admitted to hospital quite soon after the onset of symptoms, mostly because of the severe consequences of manic behaviour.

Finally it is important to emphasize that both with mania and depression there is a gamut of severity, with changes in either direction over time. Characteristically, there is a relatively persistent change in the person's normal personality, attitudes, and behaviour over several weeks or months.

3

Depression in the general population

The occurrence and distribution of depression and mania in a population may be related to a variety of factors. Such factors include a wide variety of possibilities such as sex, age, living in the town or in the country, nutrition, marital status, socio-economic background, and genetic factors. The study of these factors is a distinct professional field – the epidemiology of mood disorders.

The usefulness of epidemiological studies in depression and mania is clear. If it were possible to find certain kinds of variables in the population which were associated with a high incidence of depression and mania, they might tell us a great deal about the cause of these states. An anecdote from the 1800s may illustrate this. In the last century it was clear that British sailors often developed general paralysis of the insane, syphilis affecting the brain. This is an illness which manifests itself by memory loss, disorientation, and other mental symptoms, sometimes those of mania. These manic symptoms are similar to those which were described in the previous chapter. At the same time that it was noted that British sailors showed a high incidence of this disease, it was also observed that Catholic nuns in England were notable because of an almost complete absence of general paralysis in their lives. It was thought by some professionals that sea air might well be a causative factor in the illness. No doubt a somewhat more sceptical and perspicacious observer might have noted other differences between British sailors and Catholic nuns and come up with a more reasonable assessment of the causes of the difference.

There is another reason why studies of depression and mania in the population are important. They give us a good estimate of how many facilities, clinics, hospitals, and agencies are necessary for adequate care of this health problem. Suffice it to say that a good bit is known about the epidemiology of depression. Numerous studies have been accomplished and published.

One of the best ways to evaluate the presence of depression and mania in the population is to do a 'cohort study'. This kind of study starts with a group of people who are born at a particular time and ends with their being followed up many years later, after they have gone through the entire 'age of risk'. The age of risk is the period of time in which most individuals are known to develop a particular disease. After some simple corrections are imposed, such a cohort study ends up with a number which is called the 'morbidity risk' for the disease. The 'morbidity risk' or 'disease expectancy' is an estimate, expressed as a percentage, of the probability that a person in the population will develop this disease at some time or another during his life if he survives the period of risk for the disease.

A good example of the findings of such an epidemiological study is presented in Table 3.1.

Table 3.1

Expectancy of illnesses characterized by manias and/or depressions in population

	Men (%)	Women (%)
Manic–depressive illness	2.46	3.23
Atypical depressives	0.34	0.87
Mild depressions (neurotic depressions)	2.25	4.14
All depressions and manias	5.05	8.24

(Adapted from T. Helgason, *Acta Psychiatrica Scandinavica* Suppl. 173, (1964).)

The definition of the term 'manic–depressive illness' (in Table 3.1) is that of a disease characterized by disturbances of mood in the direction of being either elated or depressed with an accompanying change in activity to either overactivity or slowness (retardation). Attacks usually occur without known cause and may last weeks to months or years. The attacks are associated with social disablement. The 'atypical depressions' are associated with mental stress. About two-thirds of such patients who become grossly ill with mental stress show a depression or an excitement, usually the former. 'Depressive neuroses' are generally milder than the other two types of mood disturbance. They occur in the context of a stormy life with many chronic stresses. These depressive neuroses usually have fewer symptoms and are somewhat responsive to changes in the environment. It is interesting that in some studies patients have gone from these mild depressions at the time of one attack to more severe ones at a subsequent attack and have earned the diagnosis of manic–depressive illness. The expectancy is the same as the morbid risk and may be roughly defined as the number of people in the population who have experienced illness or will experience it if they live through the entire period of risk.

What is striking about the figures in Table 3.1 is the large proportion of people in the population who may be expected to suffer from these mood disorders. Because so many people are involved and also because these illnesses lead to both disability and suicide, they are not trivial public health problems. One should note, however, that these figures come from a rather unusual place, Iceland. It is possible that there are different rates for other cultures and countries, but subsequent findings indicate it is very unlikely the rates will be any lower than those in Iceland. Certainly countries which have large minority groups and unusual kinds of social stress may show differing amounts of illness. However, it is abundantly clear that other studies in other countries have shown comparable or higher rates.

A recent evaluation of mood disorders in the population of a college and industrial town in the north-eastern part of the United States (New Haven) has shown very high rates of mood disorder. Twenty per cent of the population was given a diagnosis of major depression. To this figure we may add a number of patients with minor depressions. In this same population 1.2 per cent of the people had illnesses characterized by mania and depression or mania alone. All told, 28 per cent of the population suffered from one or another type of mood disorder, a very high figure indeed. Women were almost twice as likely to have had a depressive illness. Though whites were more likely to have had depressions than blacks, the difference was not striking. Grief or bereavement with a full complement of depressive symptoms has been noted to affect survivors in about a third of males and females in a separate study of widows and widowers. The figures for bereavement are not included in the rates for major depressive illness, minor depressive illness, or patients with mania and depression in the New Haven Study. As regards social class, patients who suffered both manias and depressions tended to be in the upper classes while patients who experienced only major depressions and no manias tended to be in the lower classes. Minor depression also seemed related to lower social class.

In a study of major mood disorders in the relatives of surgical patients in the state of Iowa (who were used as a sample to represent the general population), about 8 per cent of personally interviewed relatives were found to have suffered from manias or depressions in the course of their lives, mostly depressions. What is striking about all of these assessments is that mood disorders affect a very large proportion of the population. It seems unlikely that all the people suffering from these mood disorders are really suffering from exactly the same diseases or illness. It seems quite possible that some of these mood states differ from each other in cause if not in appearance.

In Monroe County, New York, a psychiatric case register has been started. This register contains information on public and private in-patient and out-patient services to psychiatric patients. It also contains material from the practices of private psychiatrists. Of the patients who received a diagnosis of a major depression (a 'psychotic depression'), the most common type was a middle-aged, married, white female. In this study social class did not seem related to the illness.

The reasons for the usual finding of differences in rates of depression between men and women are currently the subject of debate. That women outnumber men in their propensity for suffering from a mood disorder is quite obvious. Another cohort study, carried out on Bornholm Island, Denmark, shows very similar male–female ratios to the Iceland study. Among the reasonable explanations for a higher rate of depression in women are that women are biologically more prone to develop the illness; that a woman's general role in life makes her more susceptible to it; and that a woman's traditional role is related to more of the stressful events which are likely to precipitate depression. However, there is another possibility. There may be a difference in expressivity or the way the illness manifests itself. For instance, there is some evidence that women who have depression are likely to have male relatives with alcoholism. Thus, the way the illness shows itself is different between the sexes, but both sexes may have an equal susceptibility to illness. Related to the hypothesis of biological differences is that there may be a variety of separate hereditary illnesses within the large mass of depressions and manias. Some of these influence women more for both genetic as well as endocrinological reasons. Thus, major depressions and manias may occur in a woman within six weeks of delivering a baby. Though this is not a large group of patients, these postpartum depressions obviously can only express themselves in women and may account for a small part of the differences.

When an individual becomes ill with a major depression it is very likely that he or she will be hospitalized in a mental hospital or a general hospital. However, attempts to evaluate this possibility have revealed that between 30 and 40 per cent of patients are never admitted to any hospital at all, even though they may be quite incapacitated. Some visit family practitioners and some go to social agencies, but no doubt a large number are seen by no professional and live through their depressions with no help of any consequence.

Because mood disorders are remitting ilnesses, such patients do not accumulate in state hospitals. Thus, they are quite different from patients with schizophrenia, who have chronic disabilities and are not able to function in the outside world. Patients with depression and manias become ill and get well and often return to their previous state of functioning. Therefore they do not comprise a very large proportion of the people that are seen in hospitals that cater to chronically mentally ill patients. This is not to imply that they do not have some disabilities. A recent follow-up of patients indicated that though depressives do show acute worsening there is some reason to believe that this is occasionally superimposed on a chronic state of depression. This chronic state is not bad enough to require hospitalization nor does it impair the individual from functioning adequately. Many patients, however, have acute episodes and get completely well.

The relationship between mood disorders and urban versus rural living has been a matter of some discussion. It is quite possible that people living in very large urban centres are more likely to develop depressions, particularly of a minor sort, than those patients living in a rural or small town atmosphere.

Of particular interest is the question of social class and the mood disorder. A number of studies indicate that such patients come from families which are moving up the social scale and excessively socially ambitious. Schizophrenia has been noted in some population studies to be overly concentrated in the lower social classes. This is exactly the opposite finding from that in manic–depressive illness. Here, patients who suffer from major mood disorders tend to cluster in the higher social classes. This seems to be true, however, only for those patients who have severe mood disorders. As noted above mild depressions may be relevant to both urban centres and even conceivably to lower social classes. There is evidence that patients who suffer from both manias and depressions may be different from patients who suffer from depressions only. Comparing the two groups it has been noted that patients with mania and depression are more highly educated and also show higher occupational status than patients who have depression only. One interesting point is that the entire family of the patient with mania and depression will have a superior educational and occupational level. This has some meaning as regards natural selection. It is arguable that there are some biological assets associated with the illness, and that when these assets manifest themselves, they affect entire families. Certainly patients who are in upper socio-economic strata are likely to request and receive better medical care. Likewise, they may enjoy many other advantages such as better nutrition, more leisure time, etc. Also it is possible that women with both mania and depression have considerable social advantages. Because of their colourfulness and drive they may marry into higher social and occupational groups. It is far too early to determine their success in the job market but with increasing acceptance of women in more influential positions this is certainly something which should be studied. Of some interest is the fact that sociobiologists have noted the phenomenon of women marrying men of a higher socio-economic level. They call this 'hypergamy' and point out that people are like all social animals; the females move upward by their mating choices. It would be important to determine if hypergamy is an unusually potent force in women with mania and depression.

Because patients with mood disorders are not chronically incapacitated they are usually able to engage in significant economic productivity. As a consequence they tend to be less often seen in clinics and more often seen in the offices of private psychiatrists than many of the patients who suffer from other kinds of psychiatric illness. Thus, anybody interested in studying patients with mania and depression is best able to make his observations in a private psychiatric hospital or even in a general hospital.

The question of the relationship of marital status to depression is a matter of some significance. An English study indicated that married women were far more at risk for depression than were single women. Here, we may have one of those problems in definition. To assess this circumstance properly it would be necessary to divide patients into mild and severe depressions, and into those hospitalized versus those non-hospitalized. Also it would be necessary to look at the more specific syndrome, that of mania, in order to determine whether marriage was really relevant to the frequency of its occurrence.

Illnesses often tend to affect the fertility rate (ability to reproduce). A child who is born with a serious metabolic disorder leading to mental retardation is less likely to reproduce because his impaired social status may lead to chronic hospitalization or little contact with the opposite sex. It was a commonplace observation that in the years before effective management, schizophrenics, though not retarded, were so poorly integrated into the community that their fertility rate was low. How about the major mood disorders? The proportion of unmarried men and women with major mood disorders is clearly higher than would be expected in the normal population. This difference manifests itself between the ages of 20 and 40 years. Similarly divorce seems more common in both men and women with major mood disorders. Likewise, fertility is clearly reduced (by about 30 per cent) in females with major mood disorders when compared to the normal population of females. It is possible that currently effective treatment may change the situation but the findings cited above are based on psychiatric in-patients in Germany who were examined between 1968 and 1975.

For purposes of planning it is necessary to evaluate the incidence of an illness within a specified length of time. A Scandinavian evaluation (in Denmark) showed that within a period of twelve months, between 0.2 and 0.5 per cent of the adult population showed a depressive state. There was high preponderance of females over males. Only a quarter of the patients had been treated in a psychiatric setting.

Yearly incidence rates about patients who are treated for major mood disorders and related clinical states for a rural and town region of upper Bavaria were 1.45 per cent. This was almost identical with a yearly incidence for the same illnesses in Manheim, Germany, 1.46 per cent. Again there was a preponderance of women over men.

First admissions to hospitals for mood disorders to England and Wales in 1965 and 1966 indicate that in major depressions and minor depressions, female admissions outnumber male admissions by a factor of about two to one. On the other hand, first admissions for mania though more frequent in women are not as strikingly different. Males show peak admission rates for major depressions at 60 years of age, females somewhat later between 60 and 65. At 65 the rates per hundred thousand people of hospitalization for major depression fall precipitously for both men and women. For the milder depressions the peak years for men are between 25 and 40; the peak year for women is 25. As the population gets older the frequency of males to females approximates unity for the depressives. In the earlier age groups hospitalized women far outnumber hospitalized men. Suffice it to say, however, that in the cases of both males and females, hospitalization for mood disorders is a very significant influence on the population and its resources.

4

How many angels can dance on the head of a pin: classification

In 1864 the French psychiatrist, Falret, presented and described an illness which was characterized by recurring attacks of mania and depression. He had been studying depressive illnesses for some time, particularly those that showed suicidal trends and behaviour, and he noted that some of the patients became excited and showed the symptoms of mania, only to revert to depression in the course of time. Another French physician, Baillarger, came to the same conclusion around the same time. In addition to noting the alternating episodes of mania and depression, he observed that some of those same people lapsed into stupor. Falret called his illness '*folie circulaire*' and Baillarger described the illness as '*folie à grave double forme*'. These observations were of extreme importance in that both of these investigators had essentially discovered an illness.

In a sense, the description of specific diseases, and the appropriate classification of them, is the true basic science of medicine as a field of biology.

Falret's and Baillarger's descriptions are crucial contributions to the modern concept of mood disorders. However, long before, Hippocrates had mentioned clinical states which looked like mania and depression. He considered them as chronic illnesses, and he saw no connection between the two of them. In 1684 Bonet described an illness which was termed '*folie manico-melancholique*'. This description implied a specific entity which alternated between the two states of mood.

But, regardless of which psychiatrist made the original contribution or the most important contribution, it remained for Emil Kraepelin in 1896 to place the illness in its appropriate context. Though it has had its ups and downs as far as popularity is concerned, Kraepelin's classification which separated schizophrenia from manic–depressive psychosis must be considered as a breakthrough of major proportions. Kraepelin noticed that schizophrenia was an illness which went on to chronic mental deterioration but that manic–depressive disease consisted of episodes of illness alternating with long periods of health. He defined manic–depressive psychosis in a very broad way. Thus, he included under the rubric of manic-depressive illness patients who alternated between mania and depression as well as those patients who manifested only depressions or only manias. He noted that mania showed the symptoms of flight of ideas, exaltation, and increased activity. He separated this state from depression which manifested itself by a sad or anxious mood and retardation or sluggishness of thought and behaviour. To support his viewpoint, he observed that in the families of patients who showed these mood states relatives often showed periodic cases of mania or depression. Included in the category were patients who were considered to have 'involutional melancholia', a depressed state which occurred in the involutional stage of life, around 45 to 60 years of age. He believed that some patients with stupors and confusions and even some patients who had marked chronic personality disorders should be included as they had cyclic mood fluctuations. It is very important to note that Kraepelin's separation of schizophrenia from manic–depressive psychosis was made on the basis of two kinds of observation, the clinical picture and the course of the illness. This classification was presented in the last century, but it still exerts a powerful influence on all thinking in psychiatry up to the present time. Without a doubt, it was a major contribution to psychiatry and medicine.

The first step in classification is to separate the two major psychiatric illnesses, mood disorders and schizophrenia. From the previous chapter we have noted that large numbers of people have mood disorders. All of these illnesses are characterized by symptoms of depression or mania and they generally have a remitting or episodic course. It seems that there may be several different illnesses that look alike and act alike within the large rubric of mood disorders. This should come as no surprise to anybody. If we simply look at symptoms, we are quite likely to be misled into thinking we are dealing with single illnesses. Here is an example of this phenomenon. If we take the temperatures of all patients in a hospital at 4.00 p.m. a large number of patients will be found to have elevated temperatures, but these fevers will be due to a variety of causes and will be manifestations of many different diseases. Thus, we would not be surprised at all to find that patients with pneumonia had a fever, patients with tuberculosis had a fever, patients with brucellosis had a fever, and that the same would be true of patients with healing wounds and heart attacks. The simple fact of finding a common symptom or even a common cluster of symptoms does not necessarily mean that we are dealing with a homogenous or autonomous illness. Quite possibly there are a variety of illnesses which will manifest themselves in a similar fashion.

At the moment there are two ways of classifying mood in official use.

The first of these is the ICD–9 (the 9th revision of the *International Classification of Diseases of the World Health Organization*) which is used everywhere except the United States. According to this classification the major mood disorders are called 'affective psychoses' which include recurrent mental disorders in which there are severe mood disturbances. 'Affective' means involving disturbances of mood; 'psychosis' refers to the fact that the illness includes a gross misinterpretation of reality as well as a severe social incapacity. Included in the affective psychoses are (1) manic–depressive psychosis, manic type; (2) manic–depressive psychosis, depressed type; (3) manic–depressive psychosis, circular type, currently depressed; and (5) manic–depressive psychosis, mixed type in which both manic and depressive symptoms are present. In manic–depressive psychosis, manic type, the individual may have a simple mania and in the depressed type the individual may earn that diagnosis by having one or more depressions and no manias. A person who becomes ill for the first time in the involutional period of life (around the time of menopause) will also earn the diagnosis of manic–depressive psychosis, depressed type.

There is another set of mood disorders which may be classified under 'other non-organic psychoses' which are a small group of serious (psychotic) illnesses that are largely attributable to a recent life experience. There are two types of these other non-organic psychoses:

(1) Depressive type where the illness may be similar to manic–depressive psychosis, depressed type, but is provoked by some kind of stress or severe disappointment or frustration. There are synonyms for this: 'reactive–depressive psychosis' or 'psychogenic–depressive psychosis'.

(2) Excitative type where stress provokes manic symptoms.

Neurotic disorders as opposed to psychotic disorders in ICD–9 are considered those where the individual may have considerable insight into his problem and is perfectly able to read and understand reality. Under the neurotic disorders there is a mood state entitled a 'neurotic depression' which may be used synonymously with the term 'reactive depression'. It is a depression which occurs after a distressing or upsetting experience. It contains no psychotic symptoms (delusions, hallucinations); and the patient shows preoccupation with the distressing event which preceded the illness. What is more, the presence of other neurotic problems may be seen in the individual who fits the diagnosis of neurotic depression. Presumably such a neurotic lifestyle would be long lived.

Additionally, within ICD–9 there is a personality disorder which is characterized by changes in mood toward excitement or depression, these changes not necessarily being incapacitating but certainly notable. Also there is a state called 'brief depressive reaction' in which depressive symptoms are closely related in time and content to some stressful event. Another clinical syndrome is a 'prolonged depressive reaction' which is a state of depression developing in association with prolonged exposure to a stressful situation. Finally, there is a group of disorders entitled 'depressive disorders', not elsewhere classified, where the depression may be of moderate intensity in which there are no specifically serious psychotic or manic-depressive features. Further, this state does not seem to be associated with stressful events which might be seen in neurotic depression.

If the reader finds himself confused over this plethora of diagnoses, he should not feel bad. Whether these groups can really be differentiated from each other is highly questionable, and to a large extent depends not on a set of criteria but rather on the general clinical viewpoint of the diagnostician.

As may be noted from the above, the differences between some of the types of mood disorder are often subtle and difficult to define in a reliable manner. The ICD–9 depends a great deal on the experience and judgement of the examiner and it allows him a lot of leeway in making a decision.

The second major classification system is the DSM–III (3rd edition of the *Diagnostic and statistical manual of the American Psychiatric Association*). This is the system used in the United States. This is a marked departure from previous classificatory schemes. The Task Force on Nomenclature and Statistics of the American Psychiatric Association made a serious and conscious attempt to formulate diagnoses on the basis of known findings in the field. Thus, there was a great deal of recourse to the available literature and facts which are currently available in the mood disorders. Further, DSM–III makes an effort to provide systematic and operational criteria for many of the diagnoses that are used in the mental disorders (see Appendix I for operational definitions of depression and mania). Thus, the diagnosis of a patient would be based on the presence or absence of a series of symptoms and items concerned with the course of the illness. Because the patient is supposed to meet these specific criteria, the ability of a physician to diagnose a case reliably should be somewhat greater. There is, of course, no way to get rid of clinical judgement, nor should anybody attempt to eliminate it. What has been done with DSM–III is to provide a clinical picture which can be used for diagnosis. Thus, if one were to hear of a diagnosis from DSM–III, one would assume that such a patient would have met the criteria for the diagnosis, the criteria being explicitly stated in the classificatory scheme.

The major heading for depression and mania is 'affective disorders' and under this rubric comes:

Major affective disorders

(a) *Bipolar disorder* (a disorder manifesting itself by both manias and depressions). A patient may be manic or depressed at the time of evaluation or for that matter mixed with symptoms of both depression and mania.

(b) *Major depression*. This disorder manifests itself by depression only. A diagnosis may specify whether a person has suffered only one episode of depression or whether he has had multiple episodes.

(c) Other specific affective disorders
   - (i) *Cyclothymic disorder*, which manifests itself by numerous periods in which the individual shows variation between depressive and manic syndromes but the symptoms are not of sufficient intensity to meet the criteria for a major depressive or manic episode.
   - (ii) *Dysthymic disorder* (similar to depressive neurosis) where the individual has a depressed mood and some symptoms, but they are fewer in number than those of a major depressive episode. Also, in dysthymic disorder there is often an associated personality disturbance of long standing which is the foundation on which the depression occurs.

Using DSM–III one can diagnose an atypical bipolar disorder or atypical depression. It is here that clinical judgement may be used. Finally, there are a couple of very specific depressive syndromes. One of these is 'adjustment disorder with depressed mood' in which the individual responds to a stressor that occurred within three months of the onset of depressed mood.

Unlike a dysthymic disorder, the disturbance is not simply an instance of a pattern of overreaction to stress or an exacerbation of a mental disorder previously noted. Also, there is a place to rate uncomplicated bereavement which should not be considered a mental disorder at all.

By now the reader is probably slightly confused about classification in the mood disorder; yet, he should not chide himself. What is necessary is a St Thomas Aquinas to arrive at the appropriate classification. The problem is simple. In neither of the above classifications is there good reason to believe that there should be that many subcategories. In fact, most psychiatrists in practice tend to adopt a simpler scheme for their thinking.

This more practical classification scheme is a bipartite one which separates a group which can be considered as 'endogenous–psychotic' from another group considered 'neurotic–reactive'. Endogenous and psychotic are not strictly synonymous but they are often used together. Endogenous refers to the idea that the illness is somehow caused by some internal metabolic abnormality. Psychotic refers to the fact that the illness is severe enough to cause a marked distortion of the ability to perceive reality and manifests itself by delusions and hallucinations. Neurotic–reactive is generally a milder illness which does not show any inability to interpret reality and is often seen in response to stressful life events. Often in a neurotic–reactive depression the individual has developed his or her depression in the context of a stormy life-style with many problems in living, for example, divorces, sexual problems, job problems, and other interpersonal difficulties.

In the endogenous–psychotic type, symptoms tend to be more frequent and more severe and often somewhat more specific. Thus, a person with the endogenous–psychotic type of depression might have serious retardation or agitation, marked guilt, anorexia with weight loss, early morning insomnia, and a diurnal variation of symptoms (maximum severity of depression being in the morning). The symptoms could include hallucinations and/or delusions. Further, in the endogenous–psychotic type of illness, the individual perceives his illness more clearly as a distinct change from his usual self and complains more often of loss of pleasure in almost all activities with a loss of reactivity to usual pleasurable stimuli. This loss of interest is not usually seen in the neurotic–reactive type. In the neurotic–reactive type of depression, the individual usually has had a lifelong history of interpersonal difficulties and develops a depressive episode within the context of the interpersonal conflict. The depressive state may bear marked resemblance to the more severe type but is not as incapacitating. Often the individual may not think of this kind of depression as being so clearly a change from his usual self in that he has had problems in living for a long period and this episode is simply in addition to that. In the neurotic–reactive depression the patient will usually be able to complain of a precipitating factor. Often, though, it is difficult to determine whether the precipitant caused the depression or the depression caused the precipitant to occur. When psychiatrists make diagnoses of neurotic depressions and compare such patients to patients with endogenous depressions, it is often difficult to separate the two types of illness as regards both the severity and the specificity of symptoms. Even though the psychiatrists presumably made the differentiation on the basis of different qualities (severity, specific symptoms, precipitating factors, neurotic life-style), it is hard to see the boundary between the endogenous–psychotic and the neurotic–reactive. Nevertheless, there is no question but that most professionals adhere to this bipartite differentiation and that it has been of some use in predicting response to treatment as well as the course of the illness.

There is another method that can be used to classify the mood disorders. This depends to a large extent on a family history of psychiatric illnesses as well as the clinical picture. Figure 4.1 shows this clinical–familial classification.

By this method we would start by noting that all categories manifest themselves by either depressions or manias and all groups have remitting or episodic courses. Bereavement is

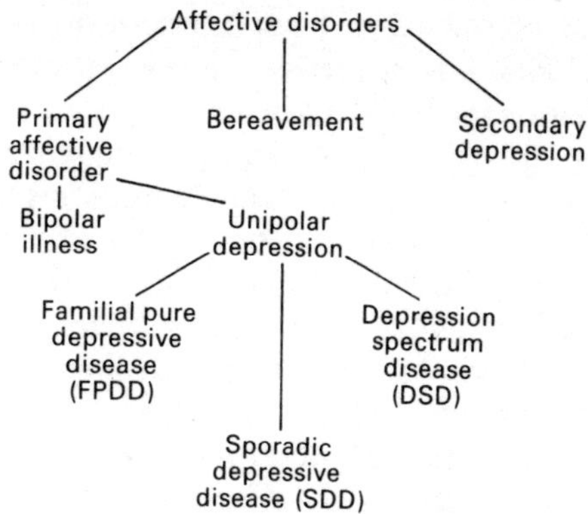

Fig. 4.1. Classification of affective disorders according to clinical and familial factors.

considered a reactive type depression. The clinical picture in bereavement is similar to the clinical picture in all of the other depressive groups. In fact, it has been noted that about a third of widows and widowers will show a full panoply of depressive symptoms. A bereavement depression, of course, improves with time.

The next category is that of secondary depression. A secondary depression is an ordinary depression that occurs in the context of any other psychiatric or medical illness. Thus, if an individual suffers from alcoholism and becomes depressed, that individual must be diagnosed as having a secondary depression. Likewise, if the individual becomes depressed in the context of a medical illness, the person should be thought of as manifesting secondary depression. In fact, large numbers of patients with psychiatric illnesses, such an anxiety neurosis, antisocial personality, schizophrenia, hysteria, and obsessional neuroses will show periods of time when they look typically depressed. No secondary mania, however, exists in conjunction with these illnesses. These patients should be considered separately from those that suffer from a primary depression. A primary affective disorder is an illness which manifests itself by depressions or manias or both in which no other psychiatric or medical illness has preceded the onset of the episode of mood disturbance.

It is at this point that the diagram branches into bipolar (people suffering from mania and depression) and unipolar (people suffering from depression only). The separation of unipolar from bipolar mood disorders was a matter of considerable consequence for psychiatry. The possibility that there were two separate primary mood illnesses, each with a specific mode of familial transmission as well as specific clinical differences was of interest to doctors. But, the most important thing for the patients was that it appeared there might be significant differences in treatment for each of the two groups. Separation of bipolar from unipolar illness was suggested in the late 1950s by Leonhard, a German psychiatrist. By 1966 through a fortuitous concatenation of events, psychiatrists in Zurich (Angst), Sweden (Perris), and St Louis (Winokur and Clayton) arrived at a similar conclusion, that patients who showed mania as well as depression had a different kind of family background from patients who showed only depressions. In Europe the two studies were based on the fact that patients who showed mania had more manic relatives than patients who showed only depression. In the United States the differentiation was based on the fact that patients who had mania came from families where far more mood disorders existed than in the families of the unipolar patients. This arose from the fact that two generations of mood disorders were far more frequently seen in families of the manic patients than in the families of depressive patients. Thus, following a systematic progression, Falret's description of manic–depressive illness led to Kraepelin's separation of this illness from the other major psychosis, schizophrenia; and Kraepelin's separation led to a splitting of manic–depressive psychosis into the bipolar and unipolar types.

Bipolar illness manifests itself by manias and depression whereas unipolar illness manifests itself by depressions only. There are familial differences between these two groups. The bipolar patient is more likely to have relatives with mania and also more likely to have relatives with depression and also more likely to have a very wide family history of mood disorder. This will be discussed at some length in the next chapter on heredity. The unipolar patient shows only depressions. He has no family history of mania. Unipolar depression can be divided into three subgroups on the basis of a family background. Some patients with unipolar illness have no family history of any psychiatric disease in a first-degree family member. Thus, that person is considered to have 'sporadic depressive disease'. Another group of patients would have a family history of alcoholism in a first-degree family member. In this group, another first-degree family member may or may not have a depression. However, no family member in this group can have mania. This illness which is identified by virtue of the fact that it has a family history of alcoholism is called 'depression spectrum disease'. Why is it called depression spectrum disease? Because, in such a family the females would be likely candidates for depression and the ill males likely would be alcoholics. The spectrum, then, refers to the family rather than to the individual. Finally, there is a third group which is called 'familial pure depressive disease'. A person with familial pure depressive disease has a depression of an ordinary sort; however, in his family there is simple depressive illness but no mania or alcoholism. Thus the 'pure' in the term refers to the familial make-up.

As regards this branching diagram one should note one specific thing about the secondary depressions. They have no counterpart in mania. Numerous attempts to indicate a mania which occurs in the context of another psychiatric disease such as anxiety neurosis or alcoholism or anything else have failed. On the other hand, a secondary mania could exist as a metabolic response to a particular drug or illness of a medical sort. Thus, in thyroid disease or in syphilis of the central nervous system, manic symptoms have been reported. Suffice it to say that secondary depression related to medical illness is different from the secondary depression related to psychiatric illness and no secondary mania exists which is secondary to psychiatric illness.

No doubt the reader will ask why so much attention is given to classification. The answer is quite simple. The effective practice of all medicine is a function of appropriate classification. Countless patients may suffer from a variety of infections. Many of the symptoms may be the same. However, there will be important differences between the various infectious diseases. Classification is necessary in order to give an appropriate antibiotic or to appropriately evaluate other treatments. Likewise, heart pathology must be classified and appended to signs and symptoms. Only in this way can a rational and specific treatment be planned. The same is true for the mood disorders. Without an appropriate and correct classification, it is highly unlikely that we will achieve the kind of specificity in treatment that is an absolute necessity for effective management of cases. What must be noted about classification in psychiatry is that it depends on the clinical picture, course of disease, and family background – but it does not have as full a set of criteria as other branches of medicine. In other branches of medicine these criteria often include laboratory test results which can be useful in determining specificity of illness. However, as will be described in Chapter 10, one of the exciting new developments in psychiatry is the possibility of using specific laboratory tests to classify psychiatric illnesses.

5

Familial background and heredity

In the spring of 1880 a rather unusual writer, V. N. Garshin, visited Yasnaya Polyana. The Tolstoy family apparently did not consider him as ill, rather as a fellow with peculiar eccentricities. During the visit, Garshin joked and talked in an excessive and colourful way. He commanded the entire evening with his fascinating accounts of observations of war. He talked constantly and fluently and, in retrospect, it seemed that if there was any sign of illness it would be this overproduction of speech. Following a subsequent visit a few days later, he was noted to be talking to himself and making strange gestures. Later that year, Garshin entered a psychiatric hospital.

In 1882 and 1885, he published two books of stories. Tolstoy himself thought very highly of Garshin's ability. A year before his death, the Tolstoy family saw Garshin at their home in Moscow. He was silent and morose. He had written very little and complained bitterly about the fact that work gave him a headache and made him feel sluggish. At the time of his visit to the Tolstoy country home, his eyes had been alive and glowing. When last seen, his eyes seemed sad and lacked their previous brilliance. He died shortly after that visit.

In discussing family studies and heredity in mood disorders, it is necessary to start with homogenous patient groups. As far as we can tell, in the house at Yasnaya Polyana, Tolstoy showed only a unipolar depression. Garshin, on the other hand, may very well have suffered from a bipolar illness in that when he was first seen he appeared to be overtalkative with a possible flight of ideas and an elated mood; but when last seen, he appeared to be dull and depressed. Modern family studies of mood disorders must take these differences into account. Groups of patients that clinically appear similar to

Garshin (bipolar) must be studied independently of patients who look more like Tolstoy (unipolar). Of considerable interest is the fact that up to 1966 when bipolar and unipolar illnesses were separated clearly, most studies of heredity paid no attention to such a possible distinction. Therefore it will be necessary for us to look most carefully at the modern family material. This is not to imply that very distinguished studies were not accomplished before 1966. Certainly early studies comparing identical and non-identical twins in terms of whether or not both members of the pairs suffered from manic–depressive illness were very important. Such famous figures as Slater in England, Rüdin and Kallmann in Germany and the United States, and Essen Moller in Sweden dominated the field of heredity and psychiatry for many years. They pioneered in the methodologies, such as the twin studies, which became even more valuable after the separation of the bipolar and unipolar groups was accomplished.

That depressions and manias run in families is an undisputed observation. A good example of this is the case of Mary Wollstonecraft, an English feminist and writer, who died shortly before the advent of the 1800s (see Figure 5.1 for her family tree). She was the wife of William Godwin, the radical writer, and the mother of Mary Godwin Shelley. Mary Godwin Shelley was the wife of the poet Percy Shelley and the author of the

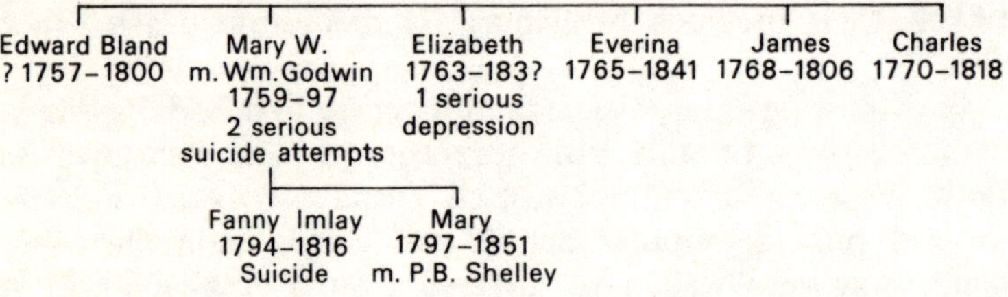

Fig. 5.1. A partial pedigree of the family of Mary Wollstonecraft. (Adapted from *The life and death of Mary Wollstonecraft* by Claire Tomalin, Mentor Books, New York (1974).)

novel *Frankenstein*. If one looks over Mary Wollstonecraft's family, it becomes apparent that psychiatric illness was present.

Mary's sister, Eliza, had an episode characterized by marked depressive symptoms early in life. Because of this Eliza divorced her husband and never remarried. She was seriously incapacitated for some time. So far as is known, Eliza never had a subsequent episode. Mary herself made two suicide attempts, one by taking laudanum and the other by jumping into the river Thames where she was fished out by some waterman and revived at a local tavern. Her first child by Gilbert Imlay was a girl named Fanny. Fanny Imlay took her own life in her early twenties.

Another more modern example of familial concordance of illness is the case of Ernest Hemingway who shot himself in his early sixties after a prolonged bout of illness with depressive symptoms. His father, a doctor, had ended his own life in the same way years before. While this is not *prima facie* evidence of genetic transmission in the mood disorders, it is extremely suggestive. However, considerable systematic evidence exists to support the concept of familial and, most probably, genetic (hereditary) transmission of the illness. First, it is important to describe the ways in which one might make observations on families.

Methods of obtaining familial information

The simplest method is to obtain a family history, which means that a patient and an available relative are questioned systematically about any kind of familial illness, particularly in this case a mood disorder. In fact, this is the only technique that gives information about a family member who is deceased. Quite likely, when a patient is admitted for care, his relatives, such as parents and grandparents, will not be available for evaluation. In obtaining a family history, it is important to outline the specific symptoms and course of the illness that are necessary to make a diagnosis. It is useful to ask a depressed patient whether anybody in his family has had an illness similar to his own. Therefore we would ask the patient whether anybody in the family had an episode of illness that manifested itself by sad mood, slowness, sleep problems, and self-derogation. We would want to know whether this impaired the family member's ability to function. Was he or she able to work during this period of time? We would want to know how long the episode lasted and whether the individual recovered. Recovery is a matter of considerable significance in a family history. As we know that mood disorders are remitting in nature, effective recovery helps us to separate these mood disorders from schizophrenia where the individual is more likely to suffer from a chronic kind of incapacity.

The family history method may be contrasted with the family study method where all members of the family are personally examined. It is clear that many relatives who are considered normal by family history will become diagnosable by family study. Thus, the family history method rates some family members well who, in reality, are ill. These are called false negatives. These false impressions can be corrected by the personal interview of the members of the family.

With the family history method, which is often the best that can be done by the clinician, it is necessary to ask about all members of the family. Thus, in talking to a patient or his accompanying relative, one would want to know about parents, brothers and sisters, children, aunts and uncles, grandparents, and cousins. In obtaining the family history, each relative should be itemized and for each relative inquiries about the presence of a mood disorder should be made. The importance of asking specific questions is clear. As an example, several years ago a man was admitted to the hospital in the middle of a manic episode. He had had several admissions before this. In each of these admissions he had been asked whether anybody in his family had had a psychiatric illness and he had always said no. On this last occasion, he was asked about each member of the family; and when the questions concerned his mother, he was asked whether she had ever been admitted to any kind of psychiatric hospital in the city of St Louis. The names of these hospitals were then specified and he told the examiners that indeed she had been admitted. In fact, she had died in a psychiatric hospital. There was no reason to believe that he had been lying on previous occasions. He simply had not put the questions together with the facts of his mother's admission and death. This highlights the great importance of specificity in interviewing. The questions should not be subtle. They should be very direct and should be very specific.

Of course, the main reason for doing a family history or family study of mood disorders is to determine whether a genetic factor is important in the transmission of the illness. There are several kinds of study which can be accomplished using the two methods described above.

Types of study that point to a hereditary factor

The first of these is a simple population study in which patients with mood disorders are compared to a set of normals as regards the presence or absence of depression or mania in their families. More mood illness in the families of the mood disordered patients compared to the families of normals suggest a hereditary or genetic factor. However, it does not prove beyond the shadow of a doubt that a genetic factor exists. After all, there will be a family clustering of infectious diseases because of proximity and there will be a family clustering of nutritional diseases because of similar diets. Obviously, in neither of the above cases does the familial clustering prove the fact that the illnesses are hereditary. The family study, though, is the first step and very valuable in deciding whether heredity is a legitimate possibility.

A second type of useful investigation is that of comparing identical twins with non-identical twins as regards the frequency of concordance of an illness. Identical twins share 100 per cent of each other's genes. Therefore, they are both more likely to have an illness which is hereditary than are pairs of non-identical twins where the sharing is at the level of only 50 per cent. In a twin study, evidence of a hereditary factor would be finding that there were more identical twin pairs in which both members of the pairs had the same illness. In contrast, fewer pairs of non-identical or double-egg twins would be found in which both had the same illness. The word for two members of a twin pair being similarly ill is 'concordance'. In a hereditary disorder, the more genes which are shared in a familial pairing, the more likely it is that there will be familial concordance for the illness. Thus, an identical twin pair shares 100 per cent of the genes, a non-identical twin pair 50 per cent, a set of siblings 50 per cent, a parent and child pair 50 per cent, and a grandchild–grandparent 25 per cent. Certainly then, concordance should be greatest in identical twins. The weakness in the twin studies lies in the fact that identical twins may be brought up more similarly than non-identical twins or other kinds of pairs. Thus, in a family a set of identical twins may be looked upon as being essentially the same kind of person and have essentially the same kind of environmental influences. If such environmental influences are important, it might be this which accounts for a significant similarity as regards illness. One way to deal with this problem in twin studies is to attempt to accumulate a sizeable number of identical twin pairs in which one member has had a specific illness and in which the twins have been separated at birth or early in life. This would control for the effect of environment on the cause of the illness.

A third very powerful technique for studying heredity is the adoption study. Adoption is a natural phenomenon that can be capitalized upon. Numerous children are separated from their parents at birth or early in life and brought up by a set of adoptive parents. Thus, for practical purposes, environmental influences on their upbringing from their biological parents are of no account. Given this phenomenon, one could start with a group of parents with a mood disorder who had put their children up for adoption. One would then evaluate the children to see whether or not they had a similar type of mood disorder. To complete the circle, one should also look into the adoptive parents in order to make certain that they are not overly represented with the same illness. In this kind of study, it is necessary to have a control group of children who have been adopted out in order to make certain that the process of adoption does not add to the risk of becoming depressed or manic. Alternatively, one could start with a depressed or manic adopted child and look back to the parents to see whether the biological parents had a similar illness or whether the adoptive parents had a similar illness. Again, a control group is necessary. One would need to take a group of adopted children who did not suffer from mood disorders and then look into the biological and adoptive parents of these children. This is an extremely effective way of ascertaining whether a hereditary factor is present in the genesis of an illness. A positive finding showing that biological parents and their depressed adopted-out children are more concordant for the illness as opposed to (1) adoptive parents and these same adoptees or (2) control adoptees and their biological parents shows beyond a shadow of a doubt that a genetic or hereditary factor is operative.

Finally, another way to study heredity is to do a 'half sib study'. Often depressed patients are related to half brothers and half sisters. They share one parent but not the other. If one looked at the half sibs who shared an ill parent and saw an increase in illness in those half sibs as opposed to the half sibs who shared a non-ill parent, it would be striking evidence in favour of a hereditary factor.

These then are the ways in which one might investigate the familial background of an illness. The presentation of pedigrees of this kind is very useful in making a decision about a genetic background.

Evidence in favour of a genetic factor in the mood disorders

A recent study in Iowa compared the number of ill family members in groups of patients who had been diagnosed as having a bipolar or unipolar mood disorder. These were then compared to the illness rates in the general population. In this case the general (control) population was composed of the relatives of patients who had been admitted to the hospital for surgery for an inflamed appendix or a hernia. All of the psychiatric patients and all of the surgical patients had been admitted to the hospital between 1934 and 1944 for the psychiatric patients respectively and from 1938 to 1948 for the surgical patients. Family members of these groups were evaluated between 1972 and 1976. The material is presented in Table 5.1.

Table 5.1

A comparison of rates of depression and mania in first-degree relatives of bipolar and unipolar depressive patients vs the normal population

Diagnostic group	Number of relatives at risk	Number of relatives depressed or manic	% Ill
Bipolar	169	30	18
Unipolar	362	66	18
Normal population	345	27	8

(Adapted from M. Tsuang, G. Winokur, R. Crowe, *British Journal of Psychiatry*, 1980)

The number of relatives at risk are the number of people that have traversed the entire risk period. This means that the percentage of illness is corrected for the age of the relative. Specifically, if a person were 30 years old and not ill, he would still have some period of time in which to develop the illness. The formula for the number of people at risk takes this into account. The 'morbidity risk' in Table 5.1 essentially tells us the percentage of relatives who are affected with a depression, or a mania, or both. The finding seems very clear. Families of both bipolar and unipolar patients contain more family members with mood disorders than do the families of the non-psychiatric surgical patients. The number of relatives that are accounted for are those relatives who were personally examined between 1972 and 1976 plus those relatives for whom a clear and unequivocal diagnosis was possible due to existence of a good record. This means that a certain number of patients were diagnosed not by being personally examined but rather by virtue of the fact that the investigators were able to uncover records of illness which contained a lot of clinical material. In looking at the table one thing should be noted. There is no large difference in the amount of familial illness between bipolars and the unipolars. This is unlike most of the reported studies which indicate that bipolar patients show more familial illness. As regards the question of mania, more family members of the bipolar patients showed this syndrome, a finding consistent with separation of bipolar and unipolar illness. More specifically, of 17 records that were found in the families of bipolars, eight of the records (47 per cent) led to a clear diagnosis of a family member having mania. Of 30 records uncovered for family members of unipolar depressives, only six (20 per cent of the records) showed a mania.

The most important point to be gleaned from the figures is the fact that both bipolar and unipolar depressive patients are far more likely to have a family history of a mood disorder than would be expected in the normal, non-psychiatrically ill population. This suggests a genetic factor in both bipolar and unipolar illness.

As noted before, there are a variety of well-known studies of twins, but most of them look at concordance in sets of twins that have not been classified according to bipolar and unipolar illness. A recent very important study has been published using cases from the Danish psychiatric twin register. The data from this study are presented in Table 5.2.

In this study 44 unipolar pairs were evaluated as well as 63 bipolar pairs. The twin register for psychiatry is based on all same-sex twin pairs that are part of the total Danish twin register covering twins born in Denmark in the years 1870 and 1920. The numbers are sizeable and the findings support the idea that both unipolar and bipolar illness are transmitted in a hereditary fashion. In both bipolar and unipolar illness, identical pairs are more likely both to suffer from a mood

Table 5.2

The Danish twin study of the mood disorders

	Concordance in identical pairs	Concordance in non-identical pairs
Unipolar	43%	19%
Bipolar	74%	17%

(Adapted from A. Bertleson, B. Harvald, and M. Hauge, *British Journal of Psychiatry*, 1977.)

disorder than are non-identical pairs. Of course, this is what would be found if an hereditary factor were important. It is of some interest to note that the unipolar group is less concordant than the identical twin group from the bipolar pairs. This has been variously interpreted as indicating that unipolar illness is a less genetic disease or as indicating that unipolar mood disorder is composed of a variety of subgroups, some of which are genetic and some of which are not genetic. It would appear that the later explanation is quite an appropriate one.

J. Price collected a group of identical twins reared apart. They were concordant in 66 per cent of the cases. There is a paucity of material on twins reared apart. This material refers to only 12 pairs, which come from published series of cases by separate authors. In all of these separated identical twin pairs, at least one member had a diagnosis of a mood disorder. It is important to note that these cases of pairs were not reported because of their having been reared apart. Likewise, they are not individual case reports, thus getting rid of a bias in reporting reared-apart twins who might be concordant or discordant for a mood disorder. In any event, eight of the twelve pairs suffered from the same illness even though they were reared apart. By perusal of the information, it is also possible to note that in nine of the twelve twin pairs at least one of the identical twins had a unipolar mood disorder. In these nine cases, five, (56 per cent) were concordant for the unipolar illness. In the case of the three separated bipolar pairs all (100 per cent) were concordant for mood disorder.

As one looks over the twin studies one cannot help noting that in bipolar cases, although at least one of the members in a concordant group has a bipolar illness, i.e. suffers from at least one mania, this is not always true of the co-twin. In a small number of cases one twin will have a bipolar illness and the other twin will have a unipolar illness. This is true only in the minority of the cases, but nevertheless some pairs exist where unipolar and bipolar illness are seen together.

Another interesting thing is that there is no case of bipolar illness and schipophrenia existing in a pair of identical twins. This statement reflects the world literature. Many distinguished studies of twins were made long before the bipolar–unipolar dichotomy was suggested. Neither before nor after the advent of this finding has there been a case where bipolar illness and schizophrenia coexist in an identical twin pair. There are some cases where one twin has schizophrenia and the other has a depression. Often this depression has been considered to be of a minor nature, but one cannot eliminate the possibility that unipolar illness and schizophrenia might coexist in twin pairs. That statement is simply not true of bipolar illness and schizophrenia.

Adoption studies in the mood disorders are few and far between. A recent one started with 29 patients who had been adopted and also had bipolar illness. The biological parents of these adoptees were compared to the parents of bipolar patients who were not adopted and parents of a group of adoptees who were normal. Eighteen per cent of the bipolar adoptees' biological parents themselves had a mood disorder as opposed to only 7 per cent of the adoptive parents of these same bipolar adoptecs. Thus, though the bipolar adoptees wcre reared apart from their biological parents, there was, nevertheless, a great deal of concordance for the same illness. As would be expected with a genetically transmitted disease, the adoptive parents were not overly susceptible to having a mood disorder. The parents of the bipolar non-adoptees had mood disorders in 16 per cent of the cases, quite a similar figure to the 18 per cent in the biological parents of the bipolar adoptees. The adoptive parents of the normal adoptees were ill in 4 per cent of the cases; their biological parents were ill in 1 per cent of the cases. Thus, illness went along with blood relationship not with social proximity or rearing.

A recent adoption study in the State of Iowa attempted to look at the influence of blood relationship in a group of eight parents who had given up their children for adoption and who had had either a bipolar or unipolar illness. Of these eight depressed or manic parents, three of them had children who had the same kind of mood disorder. This was compared to 118 normal parents who had given up their children for adoption. Only eight of these parents had produced children who had a mood disorder. The relationship between the first group and the second group is 38 per cent to 7 per cent, a striking finding in favour of some kind of genetic transmission.

In a Danish study of the incidence of suicide in biological relatives of adoptees who had either a bipolar or a unipolar mood disorder, it was found that almost 4 per cent had committed suicide. This rate was six times higher than the rate of suicide in the adoptive relatives of the depressed adoptees. There was a group of control adoptees who did not have any kind of mood disorder. Their biological relatives and their adoptive relatives showed far lower suicide rates than the biological relatives of the mood disordered adoptees; biological relatives of the depressed adoptees had six to thirteen times more suicide than either of those two groups. A suicide is not an absolute indication of a mood disorder, but it is a common consequence of a depression. Such findings as those which are reported above are highly in favour of a genetic or hereditary cause for the illness.

A German study of half brothers and half sisters of manic-depressive patients was reported in the early 1920s. Illness in these half siblings was very high if the shared biological parent was ill. If the shared parent was well, illness was much lower in the half brothers and sisters.

Finally, there are two other kinds of genetic study which are very complex, but should be mentioned. The first of these is an association study where a group of patients with mood disorders are compared to a group of controls as regards the presence of certain kinds of genetic trait. If a known genetic trait is more frequent in the depressed patients than in the controls, it would indicate some kind of association between the mood disorder and the genetic trait, thus clearly implying a hereditary factor. The rationale behind this is related to the Euclidean axiom 'things equal to the same thing are equal to each other'. Association of mood disorder with a known genetic trait automatically means the mood disorder is genetic also. A variety of such studies have been made, but there have been conflicting results. A number of studies have indicated that type 0 blood is more frequently seen in patients with serious depressions or bipolar disorders than in the normal population. Other studies do not support this and at the present time no final answer is possible. There is a positive finding of an association between type 0 blood and peptic ulcer and this seems to be well founded. It looks as if this association is far stronger and far more constant than the association of type 0 blood and serious mood disorder.

There is an even more specific kind of genetic study. This is called 'linkage'. Linkage is said to occur when two gene locations are so close that even though each is responsible for a separate trait, their closeness on the chromosome would cause them to cling together in a dependent fashion. The proof of linkage of two gene locations depends on highly sophisticated and complex mathematics. Unlike association, one would not expect to find two genetic traits going together in a population, only in a family. Thus, the study of linkage is the study of a set of families that show both mood disorders and another clearly observable genetic trait. The most complete work that has been done on linkage in psychiatry was based on the fact that a number of bipolar families were reported where there was no father-to-son transmission of illness. This is a hallmark of X-linkage. X-linkage means that the location of the gene is on the X-chromosome, also called the sex chromosome. A father can only contribute his X chromosome to a daughter; to a son he gives his Y chromosome. A woman, who has two X chromosomes (in contrast to a man who has only one), would be roughly twice as likely as a man to have an illness which is carried by a gene on the X chromosome. There seems to be clear evidence that women are more likely to be ill with either bipolar or unipolar illness than men and, consequently, X-linkage has been invoked as a possible type of genetic transmission. There is a very good marker on the X chromosome, that of colour blindness, and some studies have shown clear linkage between the colour blindness location on the X chromosome and bipolar illness. Thus in a family, if X-linkage were to occur, all people who had colour blindness would be either well or ill; whereas, if X-linkage were not to occur, there would be equal numbers of well and ill people in the colour-blind group. At the moment, all we can say is that a number of families have been studied and the conclusions are still up in the air. Considerable data suggest linkage of bipolar illness with the colour-blindness location; but on the other hand there are other data which make this kind of finding questionable. The most judicious evaluation of the information at the present would lead one to believe that there is more than one kind of transmission in bipolar illness. One type of transmission in bipolar illness may be X-linked; the location of the bipolar gene being quite close on the X chromosome to the colour-blindness location. The other kind of transmission is not X-linked. This is not such an unusual thing in biology and medicine. There are a number of human genetic traits and illnesses which have varying kinds of genetic transmission. One of these is retinitis pigmentosa, an eye disease, which is sometimes X-linked and sometimes not X-linked. It is only in bipolar illness that X-linkage has been considered in any depth. Unipolar illness seems clearly not to be X-linked, even though there is an excess of females over males, as one sees also in bipolar illness. The finding of a linkage between bipolar illness and a known marker on the X chromosome is extremely important. Not only would it prove the presence of an hereditary factor but it would assign the genetic locus of bipolar illness to a specific chromosome.

In conclusion, it is certainly possible to say that the evidence for a genetic or hereditary factor in both bipolar and unipolar illnesses is overwhelming. The specific or exact kind of genetic transmission is as yet open to question. If, however, an illness is genetic, it indicates that a good part of the cause may be found in biological factors. Again, this is simply a case of the Euclidean axiom's being applied to the evidence. Genetic transmission is biological and if there is genetic transmission then the proximal cause of the illness must also be biological. This does not of course imply that psychosocial factors have no relevance at all. What it does mean is that there is overwhelming evidence of a biological factor, with or without a psychosocial background. Heredity must express itself biochemically.

6

The natural history of mood disorders

All human conditions, including mental ones, have a natural history. This includes the onset of the illness, whether the onset is sudden or prolonged, and at what age it first occurs. It includes the evolution of the symptoms, their appearance and disappearance. Natural history encompasses what will happen in the future. Will the person ever have a recurrence? Will the person get completely well? Will the person suffer from minor symptoms, but nevertheless function? Will the person ever have to enter a hospital again or ever have to seek treatment again? These are just a sample of the questions which may be answered by a sound knowledge of the natural history of the illness. A perfectly good example of what we mean by the natural history might be seen in lobar pneumonia which is an acute infectious disease affecting the lungs. Pneumonia begins suddenly and is accompanied by a pain in the chest. Chills and high fever are noted. A cough occurs and the patient may bring up a rusty kind of sputum. The outcome was of three types in years gone by. Some patients progressed to death, others had a sudden disappearance of symptoms, and still others had a slower, more gradual improvement. That was the picture and the progression of pneumonia in the past. Now that there is an effective treatment, of course, the natural history has been altered. Far fewer people die of pneumonia.

Of course, similar changes have occurred in the progression that is seen in the mood disorders. Effective treatment has changed many things, and, as a consequence, we rarely see an unmodified course any more. Also, as we have noted from the chapters on classification and heredity, it is quite likely that we are dealing with a very diverse group of illnesses. We would expect that certain of these illnesses would have a different natural history from others.

The natural history of mood disorders

Onset

The age at which an individual may develop a mood disorder varies over a very wide range. The usual period is given as between 20 and 70. In fact, the age of 20 is somewhat old for the lower limit of the onset. Here we have one of those situations where the subgroups seem to make a significant difference. The average age of onset in bipolar illness is around 30 years of age. A large proportion of patients, perhaps as high as 20 per cent in the bipolar group, have their first episode in their middle to late teens. Thus, bipolar mood disorder is an illness that often manifests itself in adolescence. By the age of 30, half of the people who ever will develop bipolar illness have already shown the first episode. The onset of manic attacks in late life, i.e. after 60, is uncommon though certainly not unknown. In the bipolar person the illness may manifest itself first with a mania or with a depression. Some patients have a series of depressions then go on to develop a mania. Other patients show a mania straight away and have several manias without showing a depression.

As it is important to determine whether a patient is suffering from a bipolar or a unipolar depressive illness, we must have some idea of how frequently unipolar illness converts to bipolar. In a couple of short-term studies it has been noted that patients who enter the hospital with a depression (and have had either none or some previous depressions) will subsequently develop a mania in about 5 per cent of cases. Usually this conversion occurs in about three years from the time of hospitalization. A recent 30–40 year follow-up shows a higher conversion to bipolar illness, about 10 per cent.

The time from onset to hospitalization is usually very short in manic patients. At first we believed that manic men were likely to resist hospitalization for a longer time than women, mostly because of being in better control of their environment. However, recent studies show that this is not true. Both men and women are hospitalized equally rapidly after the onset of a mania, generally within a few weeks.

The average age of the onset of unipolar depression is ordinarily ten years later. However, as noted earlier, there is a considerable possibility of heterogeneity in unipolar depression. The term 'unipolar' may be a disguise for a number of separate, autonomous illnesses. Thus, those depressives who have a family history of alcoholism in a first-degree family member (depression spectrum disease), will have their onset in their early thirties. The same is true of patients who have a family history of depression but no alcoholism, or mania, or antisocial personality (familial pure depressive disease). On the other hand, the most common of the unipolar groups, the sporadic depressives, those with no family history of alcoholism or depression or mania in a first-degree family member, will have their onset in their late thirties or early forties. This has been found on a number of occasions. The absence of a family history of any kind in a unipolar depressed patient leads to a later onset.

In general, those depressed patients who are considered neurotic–reactive tend to have their depressions relatively early in life. In contrast, those patients who are considered as endogenous psychotic are generally thought to have the onset of their illness in middle age.

It is this problem of what constitutes a specific illness that plagues us throughout an evaluation of the natural history of mood disorders. By looking at specific subgroups chosen because of special symptoms or special familial backgrounds, we will find that the natural history changes. When all of the material is put together, i.e. when all of the patients are considered as a whole, the range of possible onsets and courses and outcomes becomes enormous. Still, it may be helpful to recognize this and attempt to look at the subgroups in a relatively specific fashion.

Quality of onset

Onsets may be acute or prolonged. The more endogenous (more biological as opposed to reactive to life problems) the patient is considered, the more likely there is to be a relatively acute onset, i.e. a break with a normal mood or function. This is particularly striking in bipolar illness where an acute onset is more commonly seen than in any of the other subgroups of mood illness. In fact, bipolar illness occasionally shows an onset which can be dated to the hour. A specific example follows. It involves termination of a depression rather than onset, but the same kind of acuteness occurs with the onset. A bipolar patient in the midst of a depression called on a Thursday to make an appointment. He was to be seen on the Tuesday of the following week. When he arrived that Tuesday, he announced himself as being well. He said that at 11.00 a.m. on the intervening Saturday, he had come out of his depression and felt perfectly normal. Another man with a bipolar depressive illness was able to date his recovery to an important football game which he had watched in the middle of July 1979. He had been markedly depressed before that; and, during the game, his wife remarked that he was responding with enthusiasm and good humour in such a way as had not happened for the previous year and a half. He found himself in total agreement and remained well for a period of six months after that day.

The opposite of the acute onset in bipolar illness is seen in depressives who are considered neurotic–reactive. These are people who have marked problems in living and in the midst of these problems such people may show a full set of depressive symptoms. They find it difficult to state the time of the onset because they have been having difficulties for so long that they have problems in recognizing a change.

Most kinds of patient, both bipolar and unipolar, show a quality of onset which is between the two extremes. They will be able to tell an examiner that they have been ill for two or three months or that they have been ill for several weeks. They will not be able to date the onset to the exact hour or day of illness or wellness, and they will not believe that they have been ill for indefinite periods of time.

One of the ways in which one might determine the quality

of the onset is to ask how long a specific symptom has been present. For example, a patient might be asked when he started to have problems in sleeping. He might be asked at what point he started to lose weight. This would give an examiner some idea of how long the patient had been ill.

The immediate course of the episode

Once again, it is necessary to divide the patients into bipolar and unipolar types.

Lundquist observed that untreated manic episodes, lasted on average between six and nine months. It is particularly important to note that over half of the patients who show manias have had a depression immediately beforehand and more than half of the patients have a depression immediately afterwards. Thus, the immediate course in bipolar illness is a biphasic or a triphasic one. Some patients have short depressions followed by manias. Others have manias followed by longer depressions. The depressions that precede manias often last only a few weeks but on the average they last four months. Those depressions that follow the manias may last longer, up to nine months. In some cases, a short depression is followed by a short mania and then a longer depression; thus, a triphasic rather than a biphasic course. Today with mania being treated immediately, it is far less likely to see such an episode lasting for the full six to nine months. More likely, it will last a month to six weeks before it is totally under control with proper medication.

If one simply assesses the length of all bipolar depressions, (depression seen in patients who have had a mania) the mean duration of the episode from onset to improvement is about four months. However, it is more reasonable to look at the phasic nature and the alternation of the manias and the depressions. This is because the manias and depressions follow each other and inability to function in a social fashion occurs in both.

In unipolar depressive illness there is no mania and, of

course, there is no set of alternating phases. The length of the untreated depression in unipolars is similar in duration to the manias in bipolars, six to nine months. As women get older, their depressions show a longer duration. Very long depressive episodes, as long as many years, have been reported in older women. In men advancing age seems associated with more frequent episodes. Though these trends have been noted, they are not very stable and it really is not possible to predict length or frequency of episodes in the individual patient with any great degree of certainty. With treatment, of course, the episodes will become shorter. Grof and his co-workers reported that the treated manic episode lasts for about three months, the average depressive episode about four months.

How many patients recover from an episode?

An estimation of the proportion of recovered patients suffers from the problem of definition. If by 'recovery' we mean that the individual will leave treatment or leave the hospital and never return, we might come up with one figure. But, if we mean that the individual never suffers any future symptoms or minor episodes, the figure would be different. Similarly, we could take recovery to mean that the individual becomes well immediately after an episode and remains well for a short period of time, or we could take it to mean that the individual remains well for the remainder of his life. For this section let us simply look at whether the individual will recover from a given episode.

For bipolar patients large studies have given very optimistic figures. As an example, of 2000 hospitalized manic patients, only 14, or 0.7 per cent, required chronic hospitalization. These patients were seen before the era of effective treatment. Other long follow-ups from Scandinavia and the United States have indicated that only 8 to 11 per cent of manics did not recover from an episode. The above observations provide considerable cause for optimism but they are by no means uncontested by other studies. A Norwegian evaluation in the 1960s indicated a much higher rate of chronicity, 45 per cent. These chronic bipolar patients had been followed about six years.

A short-term follow-up of 28 bipolar patients (two years after hospital admission) broke the results down as outlined in Table 6.1. In this study 25 of the patients were followed up

Table 6.1

Quality of outcome in 28 bipolar patients followed for two years

	Proportion of group (%)
Chronically ill	11
Partial remission with episodes	18
Partial remission without episodes	11
Well with episodes	46
Well in every way	14

(Adapted from G. Winokur, P. Clayton and T. Reich, *Manic depressive illness*, Mosby, St. Louis (1969).)

personally and subjected to a systematic and comprehensive examination. What may be noted from Table 6.1 is that the most common evolution is recovery and recurrence of an episode in the short-term future. On the other hand, fully 40 per cent of the patients continued to display some symptoms of their illness. The minority of the patients were unequivocally well during the entire two-year follow-up period.

However there have been much longer follow-up studies where a large number of patients were evaluated, and, for practical purposes, the investigators found that chronic care was unnecessary. This did not necessarily mean that the patients were totally normal as regards the absence of symptoms.

It should also be noted that some of the above evaluations were made on patients who were not given the treatments that are used today. Newer methods of therapy may make a considerable difference to the quality of recovery. The simple prevention of episodes (by prophylactic treatment) would make for a far better picture of the future.

The expectation of recovery for the unipolar depressive patient is far better than for the bipolar patient. In a follow-up of about six years the aforementioned Norwegian study showed that 34 per cent of the patients who had unipolar illness recovered and remained totally well. An additional 42 per cent recovered but did have relapses in the follow-up period. Twenty-four per cent remained chronically ill. It is striking to note that 34 per cent of the unipolars were well in every way during the follow-up period as opposed to only 7 per cent of the bipolar patients.

In another study it was noted that three-quarters of the unipolar patients recovered socially. In fact, most of these patients had no depressive symptoms at all.

In general then, one may say that both manics or bipolars and depressives or unipolars tend to have episodic courses. The bipolars tend to have more persistent symptoms which do not necessarily require treatment or hospitalization. The unipolars tend to have episodes from which they recover without any residual effects at all.

The problem of changing diagnoses

One of the concerns that doctors have had about mood disorders is that they might develop into schizophrenia as time wore on. Also there has been the idea in some circles in psychiatry and medicine that psychiatric diagnosis is not, as specific as it might be and that perhaps there really is no significant difference between schizophrenia and mood disorders. In fact, we now know a good bit about this problem and it is clear that neither bipolars nor unipolars ultimately become schizophrenic. Given the fact that no medical diagnosis is perfect, it is encouraging to note that of bipolars only about 8 per cent ultimately become schizophrenic, and of unipolars, only about 6 per cent. This kind of precision in diagnosis should be rather heartening. Changes in medical diagnosis are often of the same or higher magnitude.

The course and number of attacks

The long-term course in bipolar illness may be evaluated by determining how many people have no further attacks following an initial episode. Old studies indicated that 50 or 60 per cent of patients had only one attack in their lives. Usually these studies simply evaluated whether or not the patient was rehospitalized. What happened in terms of minor attacks was not known. What seems very clear is that the future course is not uniform. More effective treatment is more likely to bring a patient to the attention of the professional, and, therefore, a better evaluation is possible. Such a better evaluation may indicate that the person still suffers some symptoms though not necessarily symptoms which incapacitate the person for work or social life.

It is important to compare the outcome of bipolar and schizophrenic patients. A recent 30–40-year follow-up indicated that in all areas, marital, residential, occupational, and psychiatric status, the outcome ratings were far superior for the bipolar patients. Thus, though the bipolar patient may suffer symptoms, he does not suffer from the crushing, chronic disability that is seen in schizophrenia.

Both unipolar depressions and bipolar manias and depressions tend to recur, but this is a larger problem in the bipolar patients. Angst recently demonstrated on the average that in 19 years four attacks occurred in unipolar depressive patients and in 26 years nine attacks occurred in bipolar patients. Also, the time between successive attacks systematically lessened. What this means is that in both groups over the course of years, attacks may become more frequent. At first there is a four-year period between attacks for bipolars and five years for unipolars. These periods become shorter with subsequent episodes, but ultimately become stable. The remitting–recurring course of the illness then becomes characteristic. Chronicity does not usually become the end result. However, this has not been found by everybody and certainly all patients do not continually suffer relapses. In follow-up a free interval of at least five years is much more frequent in unipolar patients (44 per cent) than in bipolar patients (17 per cent). Nevertheless, even when the patient has reached the age of 60, the possibility of subsequent attacks can hardly be discounted.

In the numerous studies of the course of bipolar illness we find the hint of a fascinating phenomenon. It is quite possible that episodes come in bursts which are then followed by long quiescent periods. What we are saying is that a patient may have several episodes in a relatively few years and then be well for several years. For some unknown reason the embers may be fanned again and the patient will develop another burst of episodes.

Though the bipolar patients have more episodes, very long-term follow-ups (40 years) show no difference in the end states of bipolar and unipolar depressive patients. Marital status, place of residence, job outcome, and presence of symptoms are the same.

The natural history according to the endogenous–non-endogenous dichotomy

As was noted in the chapter on classification, most psychiatrists separate unipolar depressive patients into endogenous–psychotic and neurotic–reactive. If one follows these two groups of patients over a period of time, it would appear that the endogenous patients have a more favourable course in the follow-up. This occurs in spite of the fact that they have more readmissions. This paradox is simply explained. The neurotic–reactive group, before becoming depressed suffered from many problems in living, neurotic symptoms, and interpersonal conflicts. Thus, the continuing symptoms of the neurotic–reactive group are the result of personality problems and interpersonal difficulties. In fact, as regards serious depressions and hospitalizations, the endogenous patients are much more likely to show these.

The natural history according to family background

We have defined a group of unipolar depressive patients according to family background. One of these is termed 'familial pure depressive disease'. It is a depression seen in an individual who has a family history of depression. This illness may be contrasted with 'depression spectrum disease' which is a depressive illness seen in a person who has a family history of alcoholism. Patients with depression spectrum disease, though appearing quite similar to patients with familial pure depressive disease when hospitalized, suffer from shorter episodes of depressive illness. In a follow-up period the depression spectrum patients are far more likely to have a complete recovery of the depression with no relapse and they are far less likely to have a subsequent hospitalization. In a sense then, they appear similar in follow-up to the non-endogenous, neurotic–reactive group noted in the previous section. Thus, a family history of alcoholism would predict a shorter depression and a decreased likelihood of a subsequent hospitalizable depressive episode. The person with a family history of unipolar depression only, the familial pure depressive patient, is much more likely to have serious depressive episodes in future life.

Some serious consequences of mood disorder

No matter how one diagnoses or classifies the mood disorders, it is clear that suicide is a consequence of major concern. No compelling evidence exists at the present time to indicate that suicide is more or less frequent in bipolar patients compared with unipolar patients. What is important is that in study after study, a grim fact emerges. Of all patients who have been diagnosed as having a major mood disorder who die, 15 per cent will die by their own hand. In the normal population, suicide accounts for only about 1 per cent of deaths.

Suicide, however, does not account for all of the increased

mortality in patients with mood disorders. In untreated patients in the 1930s, almost a quarter of the hospitalized manics were reported to have died between 1912 and 1932. About 40 per cent of the deaths clinically appeared to be the result of 'exhaustion'.

A recent study reported as late as 1976 showed that in a large group of patients who were hospitalized for depression, patients who were not treated with some effective form of therapy had a much higher mortality rate in a year of follow-up. The older the patient was at the time of hospitalization, the more likely was inadequate treatment associated with an increased death rate. This is seen in Table 6.2. Adequate treatment was defined as an effective dose of antidepressant drugs or electroconvulsive therapy. Inadequate treatment was defined as neither of the above.

Table 6.2

Mortality in a one-year follow-up of depressed patients

	Proportion of deaths in those	
	under 50 years (%)	over 50 years (%)
Adequate treatment	0.9	2.3
Inadequate treatment	3.4	10.6

(Adapted from D. Avery and G. Winokur, *Archives of General Psychiatry*, 1976.)

The causes of death in the poorly treated patient are, of course, related to suicide but this is hardly the whole story. Myocardial infarction was greater in the inadequately treated patients as was all non-cancer mortality. That the mood disorders would be associated with an increased death rate is a sobering thought and must be considered at all points in the management of patients.

In a short follow-up, six months after hospitalization, it was noted that suicide attempts were more frequent in those patients who were inadequately treated. This would be expected as suicide is associated with depression; and inadequate treatment would lead to the individual's continuing to be depressed and therefore more likely to attempt suicide.

In a longer follow-up, Tsuang and his colleagues noted that suicides and accidents account for most of the excess mortality in unipolar depressive patients. This excess in the follow-up occurred within ten years after the initial admission.

In summary, we can say that as a group the mood disorders are illnesses characterized by periods of wellness and illness. In some types, there is some evidence of continuing symptoms on which there is the imposition of a major episode. Other patients get completely well and may have no more episodes. Mortality in mood disorders is increased over the normal expectation.

7

Suicide

Suicide is such a specific and common problem in depression that it deserves a special section. As has been noted earlier suicide accounts for about 15 per cent of all deaths in patients diagnosed as having a serious mood disorder. Within a year after discharge, about 0.5 per cent of patients treated in a modern psychiatric hospital will have died by suicide. These proportions are only relevant to seriously ill patients who have been followed-up for varying periods of time. Whether or not there is such a high percentage of suicides among people diagnosed as being depressed in the general population is unknown.

In any discussion of suicide, definitions are of considerable importance. By 'suicide' we mean exactly what is meant by the dictionary definition, i.e. the act of taking one's life voluntarily and intentionally. An individual who engages in self-defeating behaviour or behaviour which may lead to death but who does not have any intention of dying should not be considered suicidal. Thus, a depressed patient who has suffered from loss of appetite and inanition and who is at death's door is not suicidal unless he says that he is not eating to the point of malnourishment in order to terminate his life. A person who is engaged in dangerous and daredevil efforts should not be considered suicidal, unless he too shows evidence that he is performing these acts in order to terminate his life. There is another set of terms which are important. These are 'suicidal trends' or thoughts which would indicate that the person is thinking about suicide as a potential act. Finally, there is the term 'suicide attempt' which indicates that the person has made an attempt to take his life. If the attempt is successful, the person is considered to have become a completed suicide. If the attempt is unsuccessful it is simply categorized as a suicide attempt.

Who commits suicide? It seems clear that both patients with unipolar and those with bipolar illness are at considerable risk for suicide. A person who is in the throes of a mania is not likely either to attempt or to commit suicide, because of the fact that his mood is elated. However, should he slip into a depression, he would of course be at high risk. It has been noted that patients who are generally manic and who have microdepressions, i.e. depressions which last short periods of time, less than a few minutes, could conceivably be suicidal during that period of time. As microdepressions are really not predictable, one would not be able to tell very much about suicide risk in a manic person who suffers from this kind of short depressive lapse. Not only do patients with mood disorders commit suicide, but so do patients with alcoholism. In fact, if one looks at the group of people who commit suicide in a community, it is noteworthy that the main diagnosis associated with suicides is depression and the second most frequent diagnosis is alcoholism. Schizophrenics also commit suicide. However, there are fewer schizophrenics in the community; and as a consequence, they account for fewer of the completed suicides.

The occurrence of suicide in the follow-up of a clinical population including manias, depressions, schizophrenias, and surgical controls is seen in Table 7.1. The controls had been admitted to hospital for appendectomies and herniorrhaphies.

Table 7.1

Suicide in a 30–40-year follow-up

	Schizophrenics	Manics	Depressives	Controls
Number followed up	170	76	182	109
Number of suicides	7	4	14	0
Number deceased at follow-up	69	47	132	37
Proportion of suicides among the deceased	10%	9%	11%	0%

(From G. Winokur and M. Tsuang, *American Journal of Psychiatry*, 1975.)

Of the 18 suicides in manias and depressions, 14 occurred after the age of 40. In the schizophrenics, four of seven occurred before 40. Six of the seven schizophrenic suicides were in males. Ten of the 18 suicides of people suffering from mood disorders were in males.

Alcoholics who commit suicide, Murphy and Robins found, are quite likely to have suffered from some kind of interpersonal trauma. Often they are excluded from the household by their wives or families and become suicidal thereafter. On the other hand, patients with depression who commit suicide are not necessarily responding to interpersonal difficulties. Rather, they consider themselves worthless and believe that continued life is unacceptable because they are such bad people.

How might we find out whether a person is suicidal? The simple answer is to ask the person. A concerned physician or person who asks a patient whether or not he has thought of harming himself or taking his life is performing a service to the patient. This is because the suicidal thinking is associated with an illness and when the individual has recovered from the illness, as he most likely will with depression, he will not continue to have suicidal thoughts. It should be noted that such questions usually occur in the context of examining and evaluating a patient for a psychiatric illness. As a consequence, it will not be perceived as out of place by either the patient or the family.

A distinction should be made between patients who complete suicide and patients who simply attempt it. Whereas completed suicides are to a large extent accounted for in the population by depressives and alcoholics, the attempters cover a broader diagnostic group. Thus, depressives and alcoholics certainly make attempts, but so also do patients with personality disorders, hysteria, and brain damage. These patients with personality disorders, hysteria, and brain damage, however, make up a very small proportion of those who complete the act.

Suicide attempts in the population are frequent occurrences.

In males, according to a Scottish study, the prevalence is 250–300 per 100 000 population between the ages of 25 and 55. Suicide attempts in males go down sharply after 55 years of age. Women who attempt suicide have different and higher prevalences, 956 per 100 000 population. There is a sharp decrease in rates for females after the age of 25 but they remain higher than the rates in males.

Completed suicide is totally different. White males are always more likely than females to complete suicide successfully and as they become older the rate continues to rise, up to 85 and older. Non-white males show the highest suicide rate at 25 and thereafter decline. The rates for non-white males are far lower than the rates of suicide for white males after the age of 45. In general, non-white refers to black in these rates. White women show totally different rates of completed suicide. The rates rise steadily to the age of 55 and then drop from 55 on. This drop is slight. Thus, the advent of the sixties is not associated with high rates of completed suicide in white women, but it might very well be in men. Of all the groups, non-white women have the lowest rates at all ages.

Suicide varies with a variety of social circumstances. Whether these social circumstances specifically affect suicides in depressives is not known but because suicides are so dependent on a diagnosis of a depressive illness, it is possible that they do. Of considerable importance is the problem of depression in patients who have serious medical illnesses. Though patients with serious medical illnesses are quite likely to suffer depressions (secondary depressions), these patients are quite different from the patients with primary mood illnesses. They are far less likely to show suicidal thinking or suicidal attempts.

Suicide rates apparently increase with adverse economic circumstances, unemployment, bank failure, and financial crisis. At times of war suicide rates decrease. In rural areas, farm foreclosures are associated with an increase in suicide rate. Often professionals talk and write about something called a 'Christmas depression'. This is supposed to be a depression that occurs around the holiday season, and if such depressions occurred one would expect an increase in the suicide rate in the months of December and January. In fact, the month of May and the surrounding months are the times when the suicide rate is highest, at least in the United States. There is some question as to whether certain kinds of occupations are associated with a higher suicide rate. Certainly, doctors have been considered to be at particularly high risk. This has been especially noted in female doctors.

Shepherd and Barraclough have recently found that people who have committed suicide, when compared to controls, are found to have had more unemployment, more sick leave, and more job changes. This relatively poor work record is thought to be a result of the psychiatric illness that was associated with suicide. Social class mobility was found to be unrelated to suicide.

Are patients with a depression reluctant to admit the fact that they may be suicidal? The answer to that is no. About 68 per cent of patients with serious depression communicate the fact that they are suicidal.

In recent years there have sprung up a series of suicide prevention centres, organizations which are available for consultation to the individual who may have problems with suicidal thoughts. In England this organization is called the Samaritans. It is highly questionable whether suicide prevention centres really prevent suicide. Certainly they are used for other kinds of counselling and may be of some value in that sense, but comparisons of towns that have suicide prevention centres with those that do not have them show no difference in suicide rates. However, treatment of depression clearly decreases the risk of a completed suicide. In a series of studies that were accomplished many years ago by Huston and Locher in the state of Iowa, the treatment of seriously depressed patients with electroconvulsive therapy prevented the occurrence of completed suicides in the follow-up. If one looks at mental hospital statistics in Finland and Norway, one is immediately struck by the fact that suicides in the hospital populations were at their lowest in the years when a considerable amount of electroconvulsive therapy was used. As electroconvulsive therapy became less used and patients were treated with various drugs, the risk of suicide became greater. However, this is not the whole story. In those same years, hospitals became increasingly less restrictive and more democratic. Of course, there is a simple way to prevent a suicide and that is to stay with the patient constantly. This restricts his activities. He may have to be restrained in other ways for his own safety. Therefore, less democratic, more restrictive hospitals may have had lower suicide rates. Few hospitals find this kind of restrictiveness appealing. Nevertheless, the patient and the family should recognize that if the patient is grossly suicidal and has a diagnosis of depression and is a male of middle age or older, he is at extreme risk of suicide. It is quite worth while to consider the possibility of a restrictive situation under these conditions. This is particularly so because if the person is prevented from committing suicide, he has a very good chance of returning to his usual productive life and it would be a loss to society if we did not allow this to occur. Thus, it may be quite reasonable to take a strong stand in the prevention of suicidal attempts in specific people. Often it is difficult for the doctor and the family to take the responsibility for this kind of close surveillance and prevention, but it seems worthy of consideration.

8

All the world's a stage: depression and the ages of man

All the world's a stage,
And all the men and women merely players.
They have their exits and their entrances;
And one man in his time plays many parts,
His acts being seven ages.

Many psychiatrists, psychologists, and educators have presented personal development in a series of stages. Probably none has done it better or more validly than Shakespeare and none has written so well. Using the seven ages of man as reference points, it is interesting to describe certain aspects of depression and mania which are particularly associated with each. There are important associations, and the recognition of these is useful in understanding mood illnesses.

The infant, mewling and puking

Harlow demonstrated that infant rhesus monkeys that were separated from their mothers showed severe defects in their social activities. These infant monkeys were withdrawn and shortly developed a stage of 'despair'. This stage was characterized by decreases in movement, exploration, and social behaviour such as play and vocalization. Something similar to this animal model of depression in infants has been described in children. Sometimes it has been called an 'anaclitic depression'. According to the latest nomenclature, the syndrome in infants is called 'a reactive attachment disorder'. It occurs when there is clear evidence of lack of adequate care. Infants are noted because of their failure to thrive. They lack appropriate signs of responsivity such as following movements with the eyes, smiling and response to faces, alerting responses, spontaneous reaching, and lack of participation in games. They cry in a weak fashion, sleep excessively, seem to be apathetic, and show poor muscle tone and lack of movement. Such infants are considered as having a kind of depression. Whether this depression bears any relationship to depression as we know it in adults is unknown at the present time. Certainly it would appear to be a state which is a reaction to isolation and lack of ordinary maternal care. As a good part of the diagnosis of depression in an adult depends on the ability to ask specific questions about mood and life changes, it is not possible to discover the relationship between this kind of attachment disorder and ordinary mood illness. The development of biological tests for depression would be one way to determine the relationship between this syndrome seen in infants and the mood disorder which is seen in adults.

The whining schoolboy

Using the criteria described so far (see Appendix 1 for a summary), it is quite apparent that school age children sometimes suffer from depression. Kuperman and Stewart have shown that 13 per cent of girls and 5 per cent of boys seen in the child psychiatry clinic would meet similar criteria. The symptoms of illness in children do not differ in any obvious way from the depression that is seen in adults. The ages of such children showing depression range from below 8 to 16. The severity of the depression was notable in that children seen originally in the clinic frequently had to be admitted to hospital for treatment. Anxiousness was a striking concomitant of depression in the children. Kuperman and Stewart describe a child who was first seen at the age of 14 for a depression and re-admitted to a hospital years later with a diagnosis of a psychotic depression. In the subsequent episode, he received a course of electroconvulsive treatments and responded well to it.

As regards mania in children, it has certainly been reported. In fact, there are some cases where a child has been followed into adulthood after having been admitted for a mood episode in childhood. It has been noted that in these follow-ups such children show very ordinary episodes of mania and depression after they achieve adult status. One of the questions which has arisen is whether or not bipolar illness can start in a child before the age of puberty. Certainly there have been children who have developed episodes of mood disorder at the ages of 9 to 11. It is unclear whether they had already entered puberty. In one case, the onset of a mania occurred in a girl who was admitted to the hospital at 11 years of age. The illness had started seven months prior to admission with depressive symptoms. Menstruation occurred 22 months after the onset of her first symptoms. Nevertheless, it is quite possible that she had started to enter puberty even by that time. Breast development often precedes menstruation by a good bit.

Finding an onset of mania in early childhood has been a preoccupation of child psychiatrists recently and there has been some indication that bipolar illness might start before adolescence. Certainly simple depressions are hardly rare in early childhood.

The lover, sighing like a furnace

There is no paucity of mood disorders in adolescence. Of hospitalized bipolar patients, fully a quarter of them had their onset between the ages of 10 and 19. Somewhat fewer unipolar patients have had an onset in these years, 19 per cent. The onsets are ordinarily closer to mid to late adolescence than in the earlier years. This early onset in a sizeable group of seriously ill patients is seen in both boys and girls.

Of a random set of patients under 21 who were seen and treated in a clinic, Woodruff, Clayton, and Guze reported that 26 per cent of the males and 36 per cent of the females suffered from some kind of primary mood disorder. A large proportion of these adolescents reported school difficulties, such as academic failure and truancy. In some cases the depression antedated the school problems, but in others the school difficulties came before the depression. It was not possible to establish a chronology in some of the patients. It is noteworthy, however, that in many cases school problems appear to be the result of the depression rather than the cause of it.

As far as symptoms are concerned, the depression of adolescence looks very similar to the depression of adulthood.

In relatively long follow-ups of bipolar patients who first became ill in adolescence, it appears that such an early onset may presage a future characterized by many attacks. However, though early attacks may be frequent in some cases, in others the illness burns out and the individual appears quite normal at follow-up. Landolt reported a clinical and follow-up study of 60 bipolar patients with an average age of admission of 18.

Of these patients, 43 were women and 17 were men. Seventy-five per cent had positive family histories for mental problems but this did not affect the eventual future as regards the course of the illness. A third of the patients showed schizophrenic-like symptoms, but because the illness was characterized by many symptoms of mood disorder as well as a cyclic nature, the patients were classified as having manic–depressive illness. Such schizophrenic-type symptoms seem to have no real importance in changing the course of the illness. About 15 per cent of the patients developed schizophrenia in the course of time. This kind of development in these adolescents is similar to what we would have expected had the patients been adults and admitted for bipolar illness. Forty-five of the patients continued to exhibit typical mood swings. Seventeen per cent of the patients were considered completely recovered on follow-up, the majority of whom had no recurrence following their initial hospitalization. Two patients had mood swings for a period of a few years but had no problems for a decade. In some of the patients, the follow-up was inconclusive. However, no suicide was found in the group. Of the nine patients who were considered to have schizophrenia in the follow-up, all were 'catatonic' which is a subtype of schizophrenia manifesting itself in stupor. It is entirely possible that some of these patients who were manic-depressive at admission and had achieved a diagnosis of schizophrenia in the follow-up had, in fact, nothing more or less than a depressive stupor.

Hudgens systematically studied a large group of hospitalized depressive adolescents. In doing this, he also collected a group of controls from a general hospital and evaluated depressive illness in them as well. Of 13 bipolars, 8 were girls and 5 were boys. It was impossible to ascertain whether there were any special types of personality which predated the illness. Of 25 unipolar depressive subjects, 11 were boys and 14 were girls. In this group there was better evidence of an unusual premorbid personality in that the patients were described as moody, obsessional, and easily discouraged. One of the more interesting findings concerned depression in the 22 control adolescents. In this group only two factors distinguished the depressed controls from the controls that were well. A significantly higher proportion of depressed controls had parents with histories of psychiatric disorder and a significantly higher proportion of depressed controls had severe medical illnesses. At the time of the depression, the medical stress was still present and in general this serious medical problem continued for the entire duration of the depression. In a sense studying a group of controls for depression is like studying a normal population. In this case the controls came from a general hospital. Thus, it was possible to investigate both depression and precipitating factors, i.e. major medical problems. There seems to be a relationship between the depression and the precipitants. However, it is important to note that in these depressed controls, psychiatric disorders in parents, particularly alcoholism and depression, were also important as predisposing factors.

As adolescence is associated with many life changes, one would expect depressions to be missed at times. Depressions in adolescents may not be as obvious as those in a person who is 40 years of age; and family members may simply attribute them to simple life situations. As an example of the kind of problem that one might find, particularly with adolescence, consider one case of a 12-year-old boy. His main symptom was intense hostility and argumentativeness in the morning. He would get up and, at breakfast, he would be unbearable. This pattern of anger lasted for a period of about six months. It was not typical of his behaviour before nor was it typical of his behaviour afterwards. His mother brought him to a mental health clinic where in the evaluation it was noted that he was contrite. This interview occurred in the afternoon. Thus, it is possible that this boy was showing diurnal variation or alternation of mood with improvement as the day wore on. Of interest is the fact that his family history was quite unusual. There were several suicides and at least one family member who was bipolar. As noted, the episode lasted six months. It disappeared and there was no further trouble. At the age of 22 when all seemed to be going extremely well for him, he committed suicide. One must entertain the possibility that the episode which occurred at the age of 12 was simply a depression which manifested itself in a somewhat unusual fashion.

An important question has always been whether the patients with mood disorders have special types of personality characteristics. This question is best taken up in adolescence. By this time, the personality should be well enough formed to be recognizable. Also evaluating personality in adolescence solves a major problem. In studying personality during an acute manic or depressive episode, the findings are likely to be coloured by the illness itself. Also, as it is difficult to tell exactly when the episodes terminate, even a study which attempts to evaluate a person who has recovered is subject to founder on the shoals of uncertainty. What this means is that it may be possible to study personality adequately only before the time that the illness had its onset. This automatically makes the study a retrospective one with all of the problems and questions that go into determining whether the findings were reliable. In any event, such retrospective studies have been done and they indicate that unipolar depressive patients are described as being shy, conscientious, sensitive, and possessed of good judgement. They were not considered insecure, unstable, egocentric, or promiscuous. Patients who had both manias and depressions were described premorbidly as being intelligent, shy, active, and possessed of good judgement. They were not insecure and were not considered ambitious, thrifty, or promiscuous. Patients who suffered only from manias, which would be a subgroup of bipolars, were active, egocentric, intelligent, rigid, self-reliant, and reliable, but not conscientious, dependent, or thrifty. The most important finding here is probably that conscientiousness and sensitivity were generally associated with patients who suffer from unipolar depressions. These traits are consistent with the findings on unipolar depressions from the Hudgens study, which was described above.

A soldier, full of strange oaths

The vigour of adulthood is characterized by special problems, but they occur in women rather than in men. These are postpartum depressions and postpartum manias.

The typical postpartum mood episode occurs within a few days after the delivery of a baby. However, an illness which may occur within six weeks of the delivery may equally be considered as postpartum. Another word for a postpartum illness is 'puerperal illness'. It is important to note here that we are not talking about the 'baby blues' which is a short period of sadness occurring in many women after the birth of a baby. Postpartum manias and depressions are major episodes of mood illness.

The fact that there are both endocrine and psychological changes in the postpartum state has generally been considered important in the precipitation of mood illness in women.

In one study of women who had had depressive episodes for which they were admitted to the hospital, only five had ever suffered a postpartum illness. Most of these women were unipolar depressives. The percentage of the women who had had a primary mood episode totally independent of the postpartum state and also had a post partim episode was 7 per cent. Other studies, however, have shown a higher risk. Thus, most women who have unipolar depressive illness will never have a postpartum episode. One investigator found that about 3 per cent of women became depressed after parturition. Probably many of these depressions were not too severe. The frequency of serious hospitalizable postpartum mania or depression in patients who deliver is, of course, even lower, probably one out of five hundred patients.

It is entirely possible that postpartum depression and mania is only seen frequently in some of the subtypes of mood disorder. In fact, in a broad group of patients selected as having unipolar depressions, there was no evidence that postpartum episodes occurred any more frequently than would be expected by chance. However, in a group of bipolars the case was entirely different. Of 12 women who had the onset of the illness prior to the birth of their last child, eight had had postpartum episodes and these were frequent. These eight women had had 20 children born alive, and in these 20 live births there were 14 postpartum episodes, 3 depressions, and 11 manias. In eight of the 14 episodes hospitalization had occurred within one week of delivery. There was a marked tendency for women who had had one postpartum episode to have another with the birth of a subsequent child. Of three women who had six children born after a first postpartum episode, all subsequent births were associated with a postpartum episode. In general, though the risk for a postpartum episode in a person who has had one is considered lower, probably around 50 per cent.

The newest set of ideas about postpartum mood disorder is the possibility that it is quite heterogeneous. Recent data indicate that a woman with a postpartum mania is likely to have more in the way of serious delusions than a manic woman who becomes ill at a time other than postpartum state. Also, there is a trend for the postpartum manic woman to have a less marked family history of mood illness than the non-postpartum manic woman. What is most important is that in women with postpartum manias there is less of a tendency for the mania to recur outside of the postpartum period than in those women who have their manias independent of the postpartum period. Thus the course of the illness in the follow-up may be better for the postpartum manic woman than the non-postpartum manic woman. This last point is very important. It indicates that a woman who has had a postpartum mania is at extraordinarily high risk during subsequent postpartum periods but not necessarily so during the rest of her life.

Though the above data are potentially very important, it is necessary for more studies to be accomplished in order to make a final decision about the nature of a postpartum mania.

In the case of unipolar depression, a strange finding emerges. In comparing women all in their childbearing years, it has been found that familial pure depressives (those who have a family history of depression only) and depression spectrum disease (those having a family history of alcoholism) patients are quite likely to show postpartum episodes. Sporadic depressives, those with no family history, are very unlikely to show a postpartum episode. It is possible that there is a difference in the postpartum episode of the depression spectrum patient as opposed to the familial pure depressive patient. The depression spectrum patient is generally a woman who has had a marked set of interpersonal difficulties and a stormy life. Having a child imposes more strain on her and quite conceivably the depression is related to this. On the other hand, the familial pure depressive patient does not have a stormy lifestyle and no unusually difficult set of problems. It is conceivable that in this case the illness is more related to physiological circumstances than to psychological ones. These are, of course, some of the borderlands of the problem; but they are very important because new information will help us to understand the nature of affective illness more completely.

Postpartum episodes should not be taken casually. A

woman who is experiencing a mania or depression in the post-partum period may be seriously impaired and not be able to take care of her baby. Neglect of the child may have serious consequences, both physically as well as mentally. Serious depression in a woman may lead her to be suicidal. Sometimes depressed women engage in murder and suicide behaviour at the same time. They will murder their infant or child and then commit suicide. Often their thinking at this time is centred on the idea that they are guilty about something and that life is not worth while. They generalize this feeling to the infant or child and even sometimes to other members of the family. Murder–suicide is by no means an unknown phenomenon in depressed women, and it is of particular concern if the woman is caring for somebody quite helpless such as an infant. Indeed, one must consider it a significant problem. Only by recognizing depression and mania can one protect both the infant or child and the patient herself from behaviour which is nothing more than a symptom of illness.

And then the justice

That depression is frequent in middle age is a commonplace notion. In fact, at one time there was a special word for this kind of depression, 'involutional melancholia'. It was supposed to be a depression which first occurred in an individual, man or woman, who had reached the middle years and was beginning to suffer major psychological and physical changes. Certainly there are many people who become ill with depression in the middle years, but these illnesses are really no different from the illnesses that occur before and after. Probably the most interesting association has been with menopause.

Menopause is a relatively easy thing to date within a couple of years and it would be of considerable significance if this phenomenon were associated with some kind of special rise in depressive illness. If we look at the suicide rate per 100 000 population in women in England and Wales, we will note that the ages 45–54 are not associated with higher rates than the years 55–64 or 65–74. The ages 45–54 encompass the usual menopause years. Thus, menopause does not precipitate any significant increase in suicide among women. This would be a case against the fact that menopause was really associated with any major increase in depression.

In a study which evaluated women who had had an independent mood episode aside from the menopause, it was clear that such women in menopause had nervousness, depressive mood, some insomnia, hot flushes, fatigue, and some trouble concentrating (only 7 per cent). These symptoms, however, are often considered to be part of the process or the natural history of menopause itself. What is particularly interesting is that during menopause in these women there was no greater risk of a hospitalizable depression than there was at any other time in their life. It is, of course, conceivable that there is some impact of menopause on the symptom picture of a patient who has a depression which occurred by chance in the period of menopause. A study of suicide attempts in women who were hospitalized for depression during the menopause revealed that such women had no special symptoms – and in fact suicide attempts were less common in this group than in other women hospitalized for depression. The case for the menopause being related to depression in any important fashion is very weak.

The lean and slippered pantaloon

There is a commonly held tenet that elderly patients are at unusually high risk for depression. This is highly questionable. The data for first ever admissions for depression in England and Wales, 1965–1966, revealed that in males over 60 psychotic depressions, neurotic depressions, and unspecified depressive states all decrease in frequency. After 60 there is nothing but a fall for each subsequent age category. For women there is a slight, but unimpressive, rise between 60 and 65 for psychotic and unspecified depressions and a fall for neurotic depressions. And, in women, from 65 on, for all the age groups, hospitalizations for all types of depressions fall in frequency. In women there is no rise in suicide rates with age after 45.

It would be interesting to discover whether there is some change in quality of depression with age. There is some reason to believe that as women become older their depressions are likely to be more chronic. This chronicity, however, does not last forever; and though the episodes are longer, the patients will ultimately improve if they survive the episode. With aging, men do not seem to have more chronicity but quite possibly have more episodes.

Minor clinical differences have been noted between elderly and younger patients. Agitation is more frequently seen in older patients and retardation more frequently seen in younger patients. Weight loss is a more frequent finding in female patients around 60 when they are compared with a group who are around 40. Suicide attempts are far more frequently seen in females who are young as opposed to those who are 60 or older. In a follow-up of 233 female patients who had a mean age of 40 at time of admission, about 3 per cent had committed suicide. In a group of 55 female patients who had an average age of 60 at admission, none had committed suicide in a three-year follow-up.

Severity of symptoms does not differ between elderly and younger women. Such symptoms as depressed mood, loss of appetite, weight loss, loss of energy, insomnia, retardation, self-blame, diurnal variation, and hallucinations are seen in approximately equal portions of both groups.

The treatment for elderly patients is similar to the treatment for younger patients except for the fact that elderly patients are more likely to have medical problems and this has to be taken into account.

Second childishness, and mere oblivion

Depressive symptoms are often seen in patients who have deterioration associated with brain damage. Also, there are personality changes. These are associated with difficulties in memory and difficulties in knowing such simple things as the date and where the person is at the time of evaluation. Such a person has difficulty doing simple calculations. His memory is poor for things that occurred recently. If one asks him what he had for breakfast or what he had for dinner the night before, he will often not be able to come up with an answer. On the other hand, often his memory for events that occurred years ago remains intact. Along with this gross deterioration are depressive symptoms, but they certainly must be considered as a different problem from the depressions in other patients who do not have impairment of the brain. Such patients are very changeable in their mood. At one point they may be maudlin and depressed and at another point on top of the world, the changes occurring for no obvious reason. There is no doubt that in very old age some patients come down with ordinary depressions. Thus, depressions in patients who are grossly intact, as far as their mental functioning is concerned, have clearly been reported in patients in their seventies, eighties, and nineties. When this occurs, the course of the illness is similar to the course in younger patients. The treatment and the management are essentially the same.

9

The biology of depression

As a genetic element so clearly emerges as a factor in causing depression, it is obligatory to accept the fact that biological differences will be found in the person with a mood disorder. The genetic predisposition must act on some biological substrate. This does not mean necessarily that all depressions and manias will be associated with some biological abnormality. It does mean, however, that in any large group of seriously ill patients with mood disorders there should be a significant biological abnormality which is not seen in a non-depressed group. In fact, it is perfectly conceivable that psychological factors might operate only within the context of a biological predisposition.

Autopsies of patients who have had mood illness have shown no clear and unequivocal findings to indicate that the brain is grossly compromised by damage which can be seen under the microscope. As we assume that the brain is the organ of the mind and that depressions and mania affect the mind, we would expect there to be a possibility that the brain would in some way be damaged. This is not the case. This does not mean, however, that more subtle neurochemical and physiological changes might not be found in the brains of patients who have mood illness. Often we get leads into new concepts by making observations of patients who have had certain kinds of disease or certain kinds of treatment. Probably it would be wise to start with these as they may be relevant to mood illness.

An excellent example of a neurological disease that shows mood symptomatology is general paralysis. This is a final stage of syphilis (a tertiary manifestation) which affects the brain. At autopsy the brain is noted to be shrunken; the changes are widespread occurring in the frontal, temporal, and parietal regions. The cellular composition of the brain is changed from normal and the presence of spirochetes, the causative organisms of syphilis, is noted.

Clinically, the patient's memory for recent events is impaired. He may become lost inside his home or in his neighbourhood and his judgement deteriorates. What is of special interest to us is the fact that he sometimes shows a picture of mania with euphoria and expansiveness. One grandiose general paretic was delusional about having received $75 000 during the Second World War from the Pope, Hitler, and President Roosevelt. Certainly, in general paralysis the mood is elated but some physicians doubt that it is typical of the mood of a manic, as it may lack playfulness. Other patients may show marked depression. All of these manic and depressive symptoms, however, are superimposed on such evidence of brain damage as memory loss, disorientation, the inability to find one's way around the house or community. One might think that as some of the symptoms of mania are seen in general paralysis, there might be some clue as to the cause of mania in this neurological disease. But, because the brain is so grossly deteriorated and is so abnormal in widespread areas, no clues have been forthcoming.

Krauthammer has described manic syndromes associated with antecedent physical illness or drugs. Some of those agents that cause such manic symptoms are adrenal hormones, isoniazid (a drug which is used to treat tuberculosis), levodopa (a drug which is used to treat Parkinson's disease), and bromides. Post-operative states and haemodialysis have been associated with manic episodes as have certain fevers or infections, such as influenza and Q fever. Some brain tumours have been associated with manic episodes and there is an interesting report that during brain surgery, mania was produced while pulling on a part of the brain called the hypothalamus. An evaluation of these reported cases which were associated with pre-existing medical problems suggests that the average age of onset in these illness and drug-induced manias is 15 years later, at 40, than the average age of onset in ordinary manic patients, at 25. Also, the family history of these cases is generally negative in contradistinction to the family history of bipolar illness which is frequently positive for other family members with mood disorders. These two findings suggest that the relationship of these induced manias is peripheral to real bipolar illness. Perhaps there might be some possibility, however, that such 'induced manias' might offer us a clue to the cause of a non-induced spontaneously occurring mania.

Depression is an entirely different matter. Patients with life-threatening illnesses or severe medical incapacity are quite likely to show a common sort of depression. In one study, about 20 per cent of seriously medically ill patients showed an ordinary depression. Whether this is induced by the medical abnormalities or simply a reaction to a very bad life situation (suffering from a major illness) is impossible to tell. As has been noted in the previous chapter, old people with chronic brain disease are very likely to show depressive symptoms, but these are usually transitory. Depression has been associated with infectious diseases such as influenza, with lowered thyroid function, and with some potent medicines. However, only one of these associations has been particularly useful in possibly understanding the biology of the ordinary depressive illnesses. Some insights come from unexpected sources and this is exactly what happened in depression.

The biogenic amine hypotheses

A drug called reserpine was used first in the early 1950s as a treatment for hypertension. Reserpine is the active principle of a plant, *Rauwolfia serpentina*, which had been used in India for hundreds of years to treat mental illness. In fact, in the 1950s, *Rauwolfia* was used in Europe and the United States as a treatment for mania and schizophrenia because of its calming influence. In animals, reserpine produced sedation and this suggested that something like depression might be occurring in these animals. What was even more important was that some hypertensive patients who were being treated with reserpine developed a clinical state which looked similar to spontaneously occurring depression. The reserpine-induced depression is not a perfect replica of a non-induced depression. The main symptom in the former is sedation and retardation of movement. The best predictor of a 'depressive syndrome' in a patient treated with reserpine is a past history of depression; and, consequently, it is conceivable that the drug somehow activates a tendency which is already present in the patient. What was most important was that part of the chemistry of reserpine in the brain became known. It depleted the brain of naturally occurring compounds which are called biogenic amines, specifically, serotonin and norepinephrine. These compounds are involved in the transmission of nerve impulses and it seemed that the lack of these two biogenic amines might be related to a depression.

Two theories involving the production of depression were formulated. The first of these was called the catecholamine hypothesis. The catecholamine hypothesis is concerned with the metabolism of an amino acid which is commonly taken in as part of the diet. This amino acid is tyrosine. In the course of metabolism after a number of stages, tyrosine is converted to norepinephrine which itself is a neurotransmitter (a transmitter of nerve impulses). The other amine hypothesis is called the indoleamine hypothesis. A good part of the work on this hypothesis was done originally in England. In the indoleamine hypothesis, the circumstances concern the metabolism of tryptophan, an amino acid found in the normal diet which, after a series of conversions, is made into 5-hydroxytryptamine or serotonin. Like norepinephrine, serotonin is a neurotransmitter.

Another observation seemed to be related to the reserpine observations and the biogenic amine theories. A drug called iproniazide was used in treating tuberculosis and it was noted to be an inhibitor of an enzyme, monoamine oxidase. Clinically, this drug seemed to produce an elated mood and overactive behaviour in some patients. The monoamine oxidase inhibitor, iproniazide, prevented the breakdown of the two biogenic amines, norepinephrine and serotonin. Thus, the concentrations of the two compounds were increased. Because of this it was considered possible that there might be some use in trying iproniazide on depressed patients. Some success in alleviating depression accompanied these clinical trials.

A set of drugs called tricyclic antidepressants were found to have considerable effect in treating depressed patients. These drugs prevented reuptake of norepinephrine and serotonin through the nerve endings, where the biogenic amines would be inactive thus leaving them free to assert their full potency at the synapse, where one nerve is connected to another.

Finally, another drug, lithium was found to be very useful in treating mania; lithium somehow decreased the amount of biogenic amines in the space between the two nerves. Thus, in a sense lithium was doing what people had observed with reserpine. It was depleting the amines and preventing them from exerting their effect. In summary, it appears that an excess of biogenic amines is helpful in treating depression and the opposite is true in manics.

It should be noted that there are really two biogenic amine hypotheses. The catecholamine hypothesis, which is adhered to more firmly by the American investigators, involves norepinephrine which is a breakdown of the amino acid, tyrosine. Coppen and other Europeans have written extensively about the indoleamine hypothesis which involves serotonin, a breakdown of the amino acid tryptophan. One of the problems with both hypotheses is that it is impossible to have a perfect animal model of depression. Consequently, research in animals does not show beyond a shadow of a doubt that we are dealing with the same kind of clinical states as are present in depressed or manic people. Also, it is usually not possible to do studies of the brains of patients with depressions and manias, and so we do not know for sure what is going on in the brain of a depressed human.

As noted above, there is no gross or microscopic abnormality of the brain. The possibility remains that there are biochemical abnormalities in the brains of patients who have depressed and manic episodes. It is not possible to investigate the brains of depressed people while they are alive because it might entail too much risk to the individual. As depressed patients commit suicide, it is possible to evaluate the brain after death in some cases. One study of suicide brains showed that serotonin was found in lesser amounts in such brains when they were compared to the brains of controls. Another study showed a decrease of serotonin and one of its end-products, 5-hydroxyindoleacetic acid in certain parts of the brains of suicide victims. The problem is that the findings have been inconsistent. Thus, one study showed decreases in serotonin and 5-hydroxyindoleacetic acid but in a subsequent study the serotonin differences between suicide brains and control brains were not found even though 5-hydroxyindoleacetic acid findings persisted. No important differences in the levels of norepinephrine have been observed when suicide brains are compared to control brains. In a third study, there were no differences in 5-hydroxyindoleacetic acid but there were significantly lower levels of serotonin in the brains of 23 suicide patients as compared to 15 controls. This lack of a consistent set of findings may be attributed to a variety of environmental and methodological circumstances which make it very difficult to come out with the final answer.

One of the end-points of norepinephrine metabolism is a compound called 3-methoxy-4-hydroxyphenylglycol (MHPG). Maas and Schildkraut have shown that some depressed patients excrete less MHPG in their urine than would be expected from a group of normals. So, less MHPG would indicate that less norepinephrine is available for nerve transmission. MHPG is of particular interest in that it may largely reflect the brain activity of norepinephrine. Thus, a finding of a lowered amount of excreted MHPG would be something quite in favour of the catecholamine (or norepinephrine) hypothesis.

Primary depressions specifically show the unusual lowering of MHPG excretion; secondary depressions (those depressions seen in the course of another psychiatric illness, such as alcoholism, antisocial personality, or the neuroses) appear to be normal. Bipolar depressions are by definition primary depressions and these patients have had the lowest MHPG excretion of all. Some of the tricyclic antidepressants particularly prevent uptake of norepinephrine. These are desipramine, imipramine, and nortriptyline. It has been predicted that those tricyclic antidepressants which specifically block norepinephrine uptake and, consequently, norepinephrine inactivation, would be especially efficacious for patients who have the lowered MHPG finding. Goodwin and others have shown this possibly to be the case. Amitriptyline, another and different kind of tricyclic antidepressant, does not block reuptake of norepinephrine but rather blocks reuptake of serotonin. It has been predicted that those patients with normal or high excretion rates of MHPG would be particularly likely to respond to amitriptyline since the implication is that the norepinephrine passageway is normal if the MHPG level is normal. Some evidence exists in favour of this prediction, though the evidence is not as good as the material on the norepinephrine-blocking tricyclics. Dextroamphetamine, a stimulant drug, produces a mood elevation in certain depressed subjects. It blocks uptake of norepinephrine. Therefore an individual who might respond in a transient fashion to dextroamphetamine might be the kind of depressive who would be especially likely to get well with a drug that blocks reuptake of norepinephrine. What we are beginning to see then is a subclassification of the mood disorders which are based on biochemical and pharmacological differences.

Åsberg in Sweden has presented evidence that 5-hydroxyindoleacetic acid (5-HIAA) is in low concentration in the spinal fluid of some depressed patients. She has postulated that there are two groups of depressions one of which is associated with a lowered 5-HIAA and is termed a 'serotonin depression'. Should there be a group of patients with a lowered amount of 5-HIAA in the cerebral spinal fluid, it would be a point in favour of the indoleamine hypothesis, implicating a deficiency of serotonin. In patients who are considered to have a 'serotonin depression' because of the fact that they have a low concentration of 5-HIAA in the spinal fluid, one clinical finding has emerged as noteworthy. These patients are significantly more likely to attempt suicide than those with normal or high concentrations of HIAA in their spinal fluid, and they are also more likely to use violent means to achieve the end. There was a suggestion in the study that neurotic depressives were less likely to have low spinal fluid 5-HIAA than normal levels.

Van Praag has shown that feeding patients 5-hydroxytryptophan, which ultimately will increase the amount of serotonin in the brain, will prevent relapses in those patients who have a lowered amount of the end-product of serotonin metabolism (5-HIAA) in their spinal fluid. This too is in favour of the indoleamine hypothesis.

Most of the studies that have been done have been carried out on relatively small numbers of patients. Not all research has supported the biogenic amine hypotheses, and though they have been around for a number of years, we are still not certain that they are correct. Also, certain types of biochemical and pharmacological interventions should make depressions and manias better or worse if the biogenic amine hypotheses were correct. The findings have not always turned out according to the predictions. Mendels has suggested that because of negative findings of this kind, the depletion of brain norepinephrine and serotonin is not in itself sufficient to account for a depressive illness.

Currently most pharmacologists believe that the biogenic amine theories are not proved. Newer work concerns the role of different kinds of receptors on the nerve cells. The response of these receptors to the various transmitter compounds is at present an active area of research and may help elucidate the neurochemistry of depression.

We may summarize these theories by saying that the two major types of antidepressant drugs, tricyclic antidepressants and monoamine oxidase inhibitors, seem to show a positive effect on serious depressions and at the same time on the amount of biogenic amines available at the brain receptors, thus increasing the nervous activity of these systems. This is the major evidence in favour of the biogenic amine hypotheses. Though these hypotheses have not been proved, they have been of immense importance in understanding both neuro-psychopharmacology, as well as brain functioning.

Endocrine studies in depression

Some new and very exciting biological findings have emerged in recent years. These have to do with hormone abnormalities in depressed subjects. Cortisol is a hormone that comes from the adrenal gland. Its production is controlled by the pituitary gland, which itself is regulated by a part of the brain called the hypothalamus. An elevated blood cortisol concentration and urinary cortisol excretion is found in depressed patients when compared with controls. Further, Sachar has shown a disturbed circadian rhythm for cortisol secretion in depressives, manifested by an increased frequency of secretory bursts and increased amounts of cortisol secreted. It is possible to suppress the cortisol secretion in the normal person by giving a drug called dexamethasone, which is a synthetic hormone similar to the naturally occurring hormones of the adrenal cortex. Dexamethasone, when given in small amounts (1 mg), will influence the pituitary to shut down the adrenal gland and decrease the amount of cortisol secreted. Carroll has shown that in normals, suppression occurs quite readily, but that in a sizeable proportion of seriously ill depressed patients (endogenous depressives), suppression does not occur. Thus, depressed patients who start with a large amount of cortisol in their blood, continue to have excess cortisol, even when an attempt is made at suppression with the dexamethasone. About 50 per cent of endogenous depressives are abnormal non-suppressors of blood cortisol. An even higher number of bipolar depressives are abnormal non-suppressors. Other illnesses such as schizophrenia or the neuroses show quite normal suppression. Patients who are considered to have neurotic–reactive (non-endogenous) depressions are usually normal suppressors. When an individual gets over his depression, his status as an abnormal non-suppressor changes and he becomes quite ordinary. It is of some interest that a patient who is bipolar is likely to be an abnormal non-suppressor when he is depressed, but to be normal when he is either manic or well.

Suppressor status has been associated with the neurotic–endogenous dichotomy of depression and also with the familial subtypes. Table 9.1 shows suppressor status in a variety of clinical groups.

Table 9.1

Suppressor studies in groups of depressives and other psychiatric patients

Diagnosis	Number of subjects	Proportion abnormal non-suppressors (%)
Unipolar depression		
Familial pure depressive disease	50	76
Sporadic depressive disease	55	44
Depression spectrum disease	41	7
Bipolar depression	33	85
Secondary depression	42	0
Mania	61	0
Schizophrenia	48	0

(Based on data from M. Schlesser, G. Winokur, B. Sherman, *Archives of General Psychiatry*, 1980.)

The classification used in Table 9.1 is similar to that which has been given in the chapter on classification. 'Familial pure depressive disease' is a depression in an individual who has a family history of depression, but no alcoholism or mania. Such an individual is very likely to be an abnormal non-suppressor. A person who has 'depression spectrum disease' is a patient with an ordinary depression who has a family history of alcoholism. Such a person may or may not have a family history of depression, but certainly no mania. Depression spectrum disease patients are almost invariably normal as regards suppressor status. 'Sporadic depressives', those with no family history of either depression or alcoholism, are patients who have an ordinary unipolar depression quite similar to the other familial subtypes. Their suppressor status is abnormal about half the time. As noted before, bipolar depressions are almost invariably abnormal, thus they bear a marked resemblance to the 'familial pure depressives'. 'Secondary depressives' are patients who develop an ordinary depression as an illness after another, more chronic psychiatric illness has been suffered for a prolonged period of time. Secondary depressions may occur in the course of any chronic psychiatric illness. It could be alcoholism or antisocial personality. Secondary depressions can be secondary to schizophrenia, organic brain syndromes, obsessional neuroses, or anything else. What is most important is that these secondary depressions are rarely abnormal in terms of their suppressor status. Manics and schizophrenics are likewise almost always normal. What we are seeing for the first time in psychiatry is an attempt to bring together two sets of biological observations, a familial or genetic finding and a laboratory finding that concerns hormone status. Far more work needs to be done in this area for more complete understanding, but it should not be difficult for the reader to note that if two biological (genetic and endocrinological) abnormalities are seen in the same person, we have gone a long way toward defining a homogeneous disease.

Other work on adrenal hormones is in excellent conjunction with the findings on the dexamethasone suppression test and the blood cortisol increases which were cited above. Bunney, Fawcett, and Davis studied nine patients who made a serious suicide attempt or committed suicide. Prior to these occurrences they had fortuitously collected measurements of adrenal hormone excretion in the urine. They compared the excretion levels of these nine suicidal patients with those of 134 other individuals who were considered as controls. Striking elevations in the urinary excretion levels of the hormones were found prior to the suicide behaviour in six of the nine patients. Thus, a person running a high urinary hormone level should be considered at high risk for suicide, particularly if he has communicated this as a possibility. As the dexamethasone suppression test is relatively simple, abnormal suppressor status (which would reflect a high hormone level) in addition to suicidal thinking might be useful in alerting a physician to a serious threat of suicide.

Other hormonal systems have also been noted to be abnormal in depression. A hormone from the brain, thyrotrophin releasing hormone (TRH), stimulates a hormone from the pituitary which is called thyroid stimulating hormone (TSH). It has been noted that there is a blunted TSH response to TRH in depression. This may turn out to be another very good test for certain kinds of depression.

Checkley has demonstrated that in patients with endogenous depression, the response of the adrenal hormone to a stimulant, methylamphetamine, is poor. Such a poor response, however, is not seen in the reactive–neurotic type of depressive patient.

What is now clear is that a number of endocrine responses are being studied. They are being appended to various classification schemes, i.e. endogenous–non-endogenous or the tripartite scheme based on familial background (depression spectrum disease, sporadic depressive disease, and familial pure depressive disease). As a result, we have an increasing ability to separate these illnesses by biological means.

It is not possible to cover all of the findings which have currently been reported. There is one more, however, that should be discussed. This is related to sleep. Kupfer has shown abnormal sleep patterns in patients with primary depressions. One of the levels of sleep is called REM sleep. REM is short for 'Rapid Eye Movement'. REM sleep is associated with dreaming. In all people it takes a certain period of time for REM sleep to occur, and the time between going to sleep and the occurrence of the first REM sleep is called the REM latency. In primary depressives, this time, the amount of time of sleep prior to the onset of the first REM period is shortened. The short REM latency is found in almost all primary depressive illnesses and is absent in secondary depressions. Thus, the psychobiological marker, REM latency, has a certain specificity. This psychobiological marker is a persistent phenomenon. It can be observed over a period of several weeks unless the person becomes well or improves. This work has been done on a large number of subjects and this increases the importance of the findings.

Thus, bringing together the biological findings, we are able to note that there may be certain kinds of clinical–familial backgrounds which are related to certain kinds of endocrine disturbance in depressives and also related to certain kinds of sleep disturbance. It may be that using these three different biological types of measure we may be able to finally deal with the question of what constitutes an independent or autonomous disease. This is absolutely necessary for treatment, whether it be psychological or biological.

Other biological findings

Melatonin is a pineal hormone which follows a 24-hour rhythm in a large number of animals. It increases at night in normal subjects, but this increase was found by Mendlewicz to be absent in three of four depressed patients. It is, of course, quite early to determine whether this is a meaningful finding but it gives one an idea of the kind of work that is going on currently in biological psychiatry as related to depression.

Abnormal sleep patterns have been noted to be associated with depression from the beginning of the description of the illness. Diurnal variation where the individual feels worse in the morning and improves as the day wears on is a type of abnormal circadian rhythm. A number of workers have found that by depriving depressed patients of sleep there is a good likelihood that some will have an improvement in the clinical picture. The depression remits. Recently Wehr and his associates noting that sleep in depression resembles sleep in normals who have been phase advanced, i.e. shifted to earlier times of going to sleep, have carried out an interesting experiment. They phase-advanced a depressed woman. They had her go to sleep six hours earlier than usual and get up at a different time. There was a two-week remission of her depression that was associated with this phase advance. They postulated that some depressions may be due to an abnormal phase relationship of circadian rhythms.

What should be apparent to the reader is that work in the biological apsects of depression and mania is a burgeoning field. Countless studies are being done and countless findings are being reported. The best of these studies are being repeated over and over again in order to determine whether they are true. Not all findings will be solid contributions to understanding the mood disorders but many will. The association of specific clinical and course findings, biological findings, and genetic findings will make for a better classification of illness in the mood disorders and ultimately lead to improved treatment possibilities.

10

The use of the clinical laboratory in depression

For the first time in the history of psychiatry, tests are being conducted in the laboratory which are very relevant to the management and diagnosis of the patient. For tests to be useful, they must be simple enough to be performed in a clinical laboratory of a hospital rather than a research laboratory. It is important that they do not require exotic equipment or unusual training, other than that received by the hospital laboratory technician.

The dexamethasone test is a good example; it can be performed in the clinical laboratory. A patient is given 1 mg of dexamethasone at 10.00 p.m. on one day. His blood is drawn the next day at 4.00 p.m. The serum of the blood is then evaluated for the amount of cortisol present at that time. If the patient has less than 5 micrograms of cortisol per hundred milliliters of blood, he is considered to be a normal suppressor. If he has more than that amount, he is considered to be an abnormal suppressor. This test may be useful in a number of ways. In a difficult diagnostic case, say in an effort to separate out whether the patient has schizophrenia or a depression, an abnormal test would weigh heavily in favour of the diagnosis of depression. A normal test result would not necessarily rule out depression, but an abnormal test result would be enough of an indication to seriously consider treating the patient for a depressive illness.

The patient's dexamethasone response will normalize when he gets well. Therefore, the test could be used to tell us when the individual is truly over his depression. A person who is treated, but still shows abnormal dexamethasone suppression, quite possibly should be considered still ill from the depression. In the long run it is possible that the kinds of patient that are separated by normality and abnormality in this test may lend themselves to different kinds of antidepressant treatment. Considerable work has to be done on this, but it is a promising area.

How else may a clinical laboratory in a hospital be used in order to help a patient with depression? It is clear now that we are able to measure concentrations of antidepressant medications in the blood. In some cases antidepressant medications work only at certain concentrations. Too low or too high a concentration of one of the antidepressant drugs, nortriptyline, has been associated with a poor response in many studies. The effective concentration is called the 'therapeutic window'. Therefore, an evaluation of the level of nortriptyline in the blood is useful in monitoring treatment. Patients often handle medications such as the tricyclic antidepressants differently. The same dose in two patients may be metabolized differently and, therefore, one patient may need a higher or lower dose for effective treatment. By use of the clinical laboratory, it is possible to determine this and make appropriate changes in the treatment.

One of the most important and specific treatments in psychiatry is the use of lithium carbonate in the treatment of manias and in the prevention of episodes of manias and depressions in patients who have had multiple episodes. Lithium can be a toxic drug if there is too much in the body; consequently the clinical laboratory must be used to determine the blood levels of lithium. This is particularly important very early in the treatment, but even later on there may be circumstances which arise that make it necessary to monitor the blood levels of lithium.

Measurements of other hormones such as growth hormone or the thyroid hormones may in the near future be very useful for both diagnosis and for the assessment of certain kinds of treatment. A sleep laboratory can be set up in such a way as to also be useful for these goals.

Radiology departments in hospitals are also able to make significant contributions. Suppose that an individual was admitted who gave some evidence of brain damage but there was some uncertainty about this. Let us also assume that this individual had a number of symptoms of depression. The important question has to do with whether to treat this patient for his depression or whether to assume that it was simply secondary to the brain damage. Computerized tomography (the CT scan) would be helpful in making the decision. A large amount of brain destruction picked up by this method would weigh heavily in favour of some kind of dementia which was simply manifesting itself at times with depression.

A clinical laboratory in the general hospital is well able to estimate the concentrations of a variety of elements in the blood and urine. Not only can it measure these, but it can also evaluate of toxic substances that might be involved in causing depressive symptoms. Often the adequate workup of a depressed patient involves the use and interpretation of these simple and widely used laboratory tests.

Finally, one other type of laboratory test is useful. If the kinds of depression which are genetic are linked to other genetic markers on the same chromosome and these other genetic markers are easily measured, it might, in the future, be possible to determine which person in a family is at special risk for the illness. We have some markers that may be linked at the present time and it seems quite possible, and indeed probable, that others will be found as further work goes on. Should this happen, we might be able to identify a person relatively early in life, and if there were reasonable preventive measures, these could be instituted. However, it should be clear to the reader that these kinds of marker diagnoses are only future possibilities. They do not exist at the present time. The other kinds of laboratory tests, though, are simple to do in a clinical laboratory and may well be useful in the very near future.

11

Psychosocial contributions to depression

To a large extent mood illness is assessed by evaluating the state of mind. And states of mind are often subject to change in response to various life events. It is plausible that this happens in diagnosable depressions and manias. The concept of an endogenous depression, one that comes from within the body, implies that life events or personal circumstances are of minor importance in the development of the illness. The non-endogenous or neurotic–reactive type of depression is presumed to be very dependent on the affairs of the individual.

We have noted that patients with a family history of depression only (familial pure depression) are far less likely to have problems in living than patients who have a family history of alcoholism (depression spectrum patients). In this sense, depression spectrum patients are similar to neurotic–reactive patients. None of these definitions or findings, however, answer the real question, namely, are life events in any way associated with the cause of mood illness?

In a sense, the development of rigorous definitions of manias and depressions (see Appendix 1) and systematic attempts to date the onset of an illness as well as the occurrence of life events have made it possible to better evaluate psychosocial circumstances in the causation of mood illness.

'Men have died from time to time, and worms have eaten them, but not for love', wrote Shakespeare in *As You Like It*. The implication was that major changes in the lives of people were not necessarily related to important life circumstances. Nevertheless, at present time there is some reason to believe that psychosocial events are influential in mood disorders; but they may be influential in only certain groups of patients; and they may, in fact, be acting on individuals who are vulnerable to change for other reasons, for example genetic background. That this may indeed be true was found in a recent study by Hays. He found that individuals with normal personalities needed considerably more psychological stress to precipitate their depressions than individuals who had significant personality problems. This suggests that precipitation may occur because of trivial circumstances in a person that is somehow predisposed. Of special interest is that in this study, the specific kinds of personality which were seen in the depressed patients bred true in their relatives. Obsessional patients had obsessional relatives. Anxious patients had anxious relatives and patients with inferiority feelings had relatives with the same kinds of problems. Be that as it may, the first question to be answered is whether a clear and unequivocal depression can result from a clear and unequivocal psychosocial circumstance.

The answer to that question is a simple yes. The best example of a model for a depression which occurs because of a life occurrence is that of bereavement. Clayton and her colleagues evaluated a group of widows and widowers shortly after the deaths of their spouses. A year and a half later these widows and widowers were re-examined in order to determine what had occurred since the time of the deaths. Using very strict criteria, 35 per cent of the surviving widows and widowers suffered from a depression. These depressions are similar in part to depressions that are seen in the clinic and in the hospital. Of some interest is the fact that the symptom, fear of loosing one's mind, was not seen in the depressed survivors. Such symptoms as diurnal variation, hopeless feelings, feelings of being a burden, were quite commonly encountered in the bereaved depression patients. Being female did not appear to predispose the widows to more depression than the widowers. A family history of depression or alcoholism was not more or less associated with the depression of bereavement. There was no difference in the number of visits to doctors or in the taking of tranquillizers in those who suffered from a depression with their bereavement as opposed to those who did not suffer such a depression. Visiting a physician for symptoms related to grieving was no more frequent in either the depressed or the non-depressed survivors. What seems very interesting about this study is that the individuals had an appropriate symptom picture for a major mood disorder but they did not act in exactly the same way as a patient who becomes depressed outside of the bereavement circumstance. The study indicated, however, that depression as we define it is certainly seen as a consequence of a psychological stress, in this case, bereavement. In follow-up it was noted that of the group who had become depressed at one month after the death, two-thirds had recovered. However, after an average of about 13 months, a third had remained depressed and another small number had gone from being well to being ill. Again, the symptoms at 13 months were similar to those immediately after the bereavement and similar to those that are seen in a hospitalized depressive patient. Again, at the time of the follow-up when one compared those who were depressed with those widows and widowers who were not depressed, there was no difference in visits to physicians or the use of sleeping medicine or tranquillizers.

However, there are important differences between a bereavement depression and any ordinary depression which is seen in the clinic or hospital. In general, if one compares bereaved subjects to hospitalized subjects, it seems clear that the depression of bereavement is less severe than the depression that is seen in the hospital. Those patients who have primary mood illness have more symptoms of depression than those who have bereavement. Nevertheless, both groups must be considered as being depressed. Such symptoms as feeling one would rather be dead, suicidal thoughts, retardation of movement and thinking, feeling that one is a burden, and hopelessness and worthlessness are far more common in the patients that are admitted to the hospital for a primary depression than for the patients who suffered the depression of bereavement. The simple fact that bereaved patients do not seek or are forced to seek extensive medical or psychiatric are makes them different. Likewise, the fact that bereaved depressives show no previous history of psychiatric illness and do not define their condition as a change from their usual selves suggests that their depression is quite different from that of the ordinary depressive patient who comes to the clinic or hospital.

Some studies have indicated that there is an elevated risk for mortality associated with conjugal bereavement. As has been noted before, there is an elevated risk for mortality in mood illness when compared to the mortality of the normal population. In a sense then, bereavement depressions and primary depressions have something in common. However, not all studies agree on the possibility of an increased mortality in bereavement.

Now that we have recognized that certain life events can be related to depression in a reasonable, causal way, it is important to look into the role of life events in the ordinary patient who is seen in the hospital or clinic for a primary depression. Paykel and his co-investigators evaluated this in a large group of depressed patients who were admitted to out-patient clinics, day hospitals, emergency treatment units, and hospital in-patient units. An effort was made to record life events and to divide them into those that might be considered desirable and undesirable. Desirable events would be such things as an engagement, or marriage, or promotion, whereas undesirable events would be death of a family member, separation, demotion, serious illness of a family member, imprisonment, financial problems, unemployment, legal problems, divorce, business failure, being sacked, and having a stillbirth. Undesirable events were related to the development of depression. This study had the good fortune to have access to a group of community controls. Such things as serious illness of a family member, death of an immediate family member, serious personal illness, marital separation, and a change in work conditions were far more frequently seen in the depressed patients than in the controls. Also there was an effort to divide life events into entrances and exits. Entrances were engagements, or marriage, or birth of a child, or a new person in the home, whereas exits were death of a close family member, separation, divorce, family member leaving home, or a child married. The exits were seen significantly more frequently in depressed patients than in controls but the same was not true for the entrances.

Similar findings occurred in a study of suicide attempters. Such people reported four times as many undesirable life events as were reported by subjects from the general population and one and a half times as many were reported by depressed patients prior to onset of depression. Thus, one of the consequences of depression, namely suicide attempt, is also associated with an excess of undesirable life events. In a comparison of recovered depressed women who relapsed with women who had recovered from depression and had not relapsed, it was found that undesirable life events were more frequent before the relapse in the first group. This occurred particularly in the month immediately preceding the relapse. It seems that the risk for depression is increased by a good bit if undesirable life events occur. Others have shown similar kinds of findings. Both psychiatric patients as well as people identified from the community who have rigorously defined depressions, seem more likely to have life events as a precipitant. Such undesirable life events, however, are not necessarily causative of a depression. In the bereavement studies and life events studies, it seems that most people who suffer from these kinds of circumstances do not become depressed. Most people experience these occurrences and have little or no problem. Thus, it is entirely conceivable that only certain kinds of depressives are, in fact, influenced by these unpleasant or undesirable life circumstances. In a study made several years ago, patients with clinical diagnoses of neurotic–reactive depression were compared to patients with diagnoses of manic-depressive disease, depressed type, or psychotic depression. It was notable that those patients who received a diagnosis of 'reactive depression', a diagnosis of a depression which is presumed to be the result of life stresses, were the ones who had a markedly higher rate of alcoholism in their families. Thus, it is possible that certain kinds of predispositions are necessary for an individual to respond to life events.

To critically evaluate the meaningfulness of life events in depression, we must know many more things. As may be noted from the work on bereavement, the depressive illnesses that are precipitated by life events (in that case loss of a spouse) are considerably lighter or less severe than those depressions which are seen in a psychiatric hospital. This may indicate that only certain kinds of depression are in fact precipitated. Again, the most important problem that we face is the one of classification. It is conceivable that there are several types of depression and that these are differentially associated with precipitating life events? In addition to this problem, there are two others. As may be noted from Chapter 6, sometimes the question of onset in depression is difficult to evaluate. If the onset is difficult to evaluate, we cannot be certain whether the depression caused the life event or the life event caused the depression. Most life events are to some extent under the control of the patient himself, but not all. Thus, death of somebody close cannot be controlled by the patient nor can a few others such as illness in a family member, illness in the patient himself, or a natural disaster. On the other hand, other life events might well be, to some extent, under the control of the patient. These would be such things as being sacked or having marital difficulties. We know that such things as bereavement cause depressive episodes even though they are relatively mild. We would not be surprised that certain other kinds of life event should also cause them. However, in major or severe depressions leading to hospitalization and gross incapacity, we still need to determine whether life events really play a part. The development of biological tests, such as the dexamethasone suppression test, is one of the areas of interest at the present time. Such a test could be used to investigate whether or not abnormal suppression is associated with a precipitated versus a non-precipitated depression. Quite possibly it might also tell us when the depression started.

What we are really saying is that it is often difficult to date both events and onset of illness. This poses a problem. Moreover, there may be different kinds of illnesses. This poses a second problem. And finally, depression could cause some life events as well as the opposite. This poses the third problem. The solution of these problems about the importance of life events in the cause of depression remains to be found.

Brown has investigated vulnerability factors in depressed women, both in a psychiatric as well as a general population. He found that maternal losses before the age of 11 were associated with greater risk of depression in both groups. Such a finding was not true of past loss of a father or a sibling. In addition, he found that other vulnerability factors were the presence at home of three or more children who were less than 14 years of age, lack of a confiding relationship with a husband, and lack of full or part-time employment. As some of these factors are more common in working class mothers, this might to some extent explain the class difference in the incidence of psychiatric disorder. As noted before, however, not all studies have shown real class differences. Studies of vulnerability through parental deprivation in early life have been a morass. Pitts and his co-workers reported no difference between hospitalized depressives and general hospital controls as regards all variables of parental deprivation (death, separation, or divorce in parents). The medically ill control group was matched for age, sex, and socioeconomic status. Other studies are positive and still others are negative. Again, the question of the classification and diagnosis looms large. Roy studied a group of female patients whom he considered to have depressive neurosis (non-endogenous, neurotic–reactive types of patient). He confirmed the findings that loss of a mother before 11, three or more children at home under 14, and lack of a confiding marital relationship, and lack of employment may be vulnerability factors. He then studied a group of patients who had manic–depressive illness (more severely ill than the neurotic–reactive group). He hypothesized that patients with an early onset of manic–depressive illness would have more parental loss in childhood than those with later onset. In his study there was no evidence that parental loss in childhood was associated with an early onset of manic–depressive illness. Likewise, there was no relationship between paternal death or separation before 11 years of age in early onset manic–depressives.

In the vulnerability studies, neurotic depressives were more likely to have had a parental loss caused by something other than death, something like separation or divorce. This poses a problem. As we have noted before, it is quite likely that neurotic depressives have a background of parental alcoholism or alcoholism in the family. Thus, they are rather similar to depression spectrum disease patients. What one might be noting is simply a general overall familial tendency to have problems due to either depression, alcoholism, or antisocial tendencies. Certainly these familial difficulties could well be related to genetic factors. Currently there are three adoption studies which indicate a genetic factor in alcoholism and three studies which indicate a genetic factor in antisocial personality disorder. These illnesses in parents would lead to a child's experiencing deprivation for a variety of reasons. Also, there is some reason to believe that these illnesses may lead to some members of a family having a depression on the basis of heredity, at least in part. Suffice it to say that we have not adequately dealt with the specific reasons for vulnerability.

To put all of the data on psychosocial factors in depression and mania into context, what is now necessary is a rigorous study of depressive illness which includes appropriate classifications, precipitating factors that could not possibly be under the influence of the patient, family history, and family study evaluations and the use of laboratory tests which might separate out subgroups. This is, of course, pie in the sky at the moment but it does not seem unreasonable to conceive of such a study's being done in the forseeable future.

12

Management and specific treatment

As all roads led to Rome, so also do descriptions of medical illnesses lead to considerations of treatment. Effective therapy in manias and depressions has been around for about forty years. Before the use of electroconvulsive therapy (ECT) in the late 1930s and early 1940s, treatment for depression and manias consisted primarily of placing the patient on a ward, restricting him in such a way as to keep him from doing something which would be injurious to his own or others' health, and providing some sedation. In a sense this might be considered non-specific management. However, in the 1940s when ECT was introduced into the treatment regimen, significant changes occurred. By the 1950s, specific antidepressant medication became available and further changed the treatment picture. In the late 1960s and 1970s, lithium was added to the therapeutic armamentarian for the treatment and prevention of manias and depressions in bipolar illness. In a sense, the last decade, the 1970s, completed the circle. Interest in psychological management and treatment, with the development of more specific kinds of psychotherapy for depression, returned. In this chapter we will attempt a systematic look at both the general and more specific aspects of treatment.

General psychological and social management

In order to alleviate unnecessary guilt feelings, to temper depressive affect, and to prevent the occurrence of major social and medical consequences in a depressive patient, we must deal with the patient in certain ways.

Considerable reassurance should be given to the depressed person about the prognosis of his illness. He should be told in no uncertain terms that depressions are generally limited in duration. It should be made clear that after recovery no mental defect will remain. The patient should know that he will not lose his mind and that he will not end up as a backward patient in an insane asylum. This constant reassurance is useful in the immediate care of the patient, but it has no effect at all on the natural course of the illness. The depressed patient is constantly confronted with doubts about himself and feelings of guilt. He should be made to understand that symptoms of this kind are nothing more than manifestations of the illness. They have no basis in reality. Such reassurance will make the patient feel better for a short period of time. It is necessary to repeat the reassurances over and over again. The general course of the illness will not be affected by this kind of help. This will have to wait upon specific kinds of treatment.

When a patient is depressed, it is not reasonable to attempt any kind of in-depth psychotherapy which will examine in minute detail the motivations of the patient. He already feels quite guilty, and such an examination of his motivation might only increase this kind of feeling. He is an individual who is given to self-derogation. He will consider his motivations unacceptable and this might conceivably make him more suicidal. After the depression has lifted, some psychiatrists believe intensive psychotherapy is useful in determining the cause of the depression and possibly preventing its recurrence. There is no evidence that such treatment prevents a subsequent depression. Consequently it would seem of questionable value. In any event, this does not pose a problem as most patients upon recovery from a depression show little interest in an extensive exploration of personal problems.

Often during a period of depression a patient will develop a marked dependency on his physician. If this should happen, it seems wise to meet the patient's demands. This dependency is often just a symptom of the illness; and as the patient becomes well, the symptom will disappear. Sometimes the patient will ask to be seen more frequently than at other times.

If this is so, it is reasonable to conform to his request. Thus, a physician might plan to see a patient for two or three short periods of time during a week rather than for one long period. The time spent would be the same but the number of contacts would be increased. Often this is perceived by the patient as being very helpful.

The physician should never agree to allow the patient to embark on significant social changes in his life during the period of depression. Often these changes are coloured by the patient's guilt and self-depreciatory symptoms. A patient might want to leave a job or break up a marriage. If at all possible, this should be discouraged. Once the patient is well and no longer suffering from symptoms, of course, he becomes a free agent and is free to evaluate social circumstances as he will. Decisions about major changes at that point after the depression are in his hands and the physician may be simply useful as a sounding board.

Often a decision has to be made about how much activity should be recommended for a depressed patient. Among the symptoms of depression are difficulties in concentrating and in thinking; and as a consequence, it might be wise to suggest some relief from the kinds of activity that involve a lot of intellectual activity. His inability to concentrate makes the patient feel worthless; and if he were relieved of this kind of responsibility, perhaps he would feel less likely to feel badly about himself. Although intellectual activities might be discouraged for the duration of depression, it seems worth-while to encourage physical and social activities. There is suggestive evidence that physical activities, such as jogging, may have some antidepressant effect. It has always been noted that physical activity is useful in overcoming feelings of tension and anxiety. Therefore a course of physical conditioning might be a useful recommendation.

Of course, the most serious problem in depression is that it is heavily associated with suicide attempts and completed suicides. Clinicians have noted that when the patient is most retarded and most depressed he may be at less risk for suicide than when he is coming out of the depression and somewhat more energetic. If suicide is a significant consideration, the patient should be in the hospital on a closed ward if at all possible. How would one find out whether suicide is a problem? The answer is very simple. Both the patient and close relative or friend should be asked whether the patient has communicated any kind of a suicide intent in the recent past. There should be no beating about the bush on this. A direct question should be posed; and if the answer indicates that suicide is a strong possibility, hospitalization should be recommended. On occasion neither the patient nor the family will accept hospitalization. Though this is most unfortunate, there is an alternative way of dealing with the situation. If the doctor has a good relationship with the patient, he may request that the patient keep him (the doctor) fully informed about any changes in his mind or status. This is second best to hospitalization, but at least it is an attempt to handle the problem of suicide intent.

Not only should hospitalization be considered for patients who are suicidal but it should also be kept in mind for patients who are markedly incapacitated and creating problems in the family. It is often very difficult to deal with deteriorating family relationships, and getting the patient away from the family might make it more possible to reinstitute good family relationships when the patient is well. People tend not to forget things which are said in anger or anxiety or depression. Should they not have been said at all, perhaps everybody would be better off. By separating the patient from the family and having him enter the hospital, such problems might be avoided.

Psychological and social management of mania is, in a sense, more simple. Manics tend to be intrusive, often irritating, and frequently exhausting. Gross mania is so unusual that almost everybody in the vicinity will accept the idea of hospitalization. Often the patient has to be brought into the hospital against his will but this is usually possible with mania. This is because the patient is involved in doing things which may be injurious to himself (exhaustion) or he may be doing things which infringe on the liberties of other people. It is clear that the time between onset and hospitalization in mania is far shorter than the time between onset and hospitalization in depression. This is because the community is far less tolerant of mania. Once in the hospital, the manic patient should be given as much freedom as is possible and reasonable. Restriction of manic patients tends to make them irritable and tends make them less willing to co-operate. However, often some restrictions have to be imposed. This is a situation where the doctor must accept considerable responsibility for the management of the patient. This management is perfectly appropriate when the patient is grossly manic.

Drug treatment of depression

Only a troglodyte would not recognize that pharmacotherapy is the preferred treatment of depression. Drug therapy is a rational kind of treatment and there are cogent theories as to why it may work. This makes it appear more 'scientific' and thus appeals to both the patient and the doctor. In fact, we are now seeing patients talk about suffering from 'chemical depressions' or 'genetic depressions'. The implication is clear. If there is a biological factor in their illness, they would expect a biological rather than a psychological treatment for it; and, of course, this reflects exactly what has been happening. Essentially, drug treatment of depression has taken the field by storm.

There are three major groups of drugs in the treatment of depression. These are the tricyclic antidepressants, the monoamine oxidase inhibitors, and lithium carbonate. The tricyclic antidepressants are the most used by far. The monoamine oxidase inhibitors are often employed if the tricyclics do not appear to be working. Lithium is often used for a patient who has experienced multiple depressions and manias and in whom it is useful as a preventive agent.

The tricyclic antidepressants presumably work by blocking

reuptake of the neurotransmitters serotonin and norepinephrine at the synapses between two nerve cells. The synapse is the area where one nerve cell transmits an impulse to another nerve cell. Therefore, it is a kind of electrical or chemical connection. The reason the drugs are called tricyclics is that each of them contains three chemical rings. Thus, the name derives from their chemical structure. The most commonly used drugs are amitriptyline, nortriptyline (which is the first metabolic product of amitriptyline), imipramine, desipramine, (which is the first metabolic product of imipramine), doxepin, and protriptyline. The drugs differ in their specific ability to prevent reuptake of the different neurotransmitters. Thus, amitriptyline is a good preventer of reuptake of serotonin; whereas desipramine is a very good preventer of the reuptake norepinephrine. Some of the drugs are more sedative than others. Amitriptyline and doxepin have this quality. Thus, a person who is very agitated might be considered as a candidate for amitriptyline or doxepin. As may be noted from the chapter on the biology of depression, the differential effect on reuptake may be translated into treatment. If, in fact, there are serotonin depressions which are different from norepinephrine depressions, different drugs might be used. Thus, a failure with one tricyclic may simply indicate the need to try a different one that has a different effect on reuptake. Newer medicines are on the market that have very specific effects on neurotransmitters. These include clomipramine, a potent serotonin uptake inhibitor, maprotiline, and viloxazine. The usual drugs which are given, however, remain imipramine, amitriptyline, desipramine, nortriptyline, and doxepin. These drugs are usually given at the beginning of therapy at about the level of 75 mg daily, most often in divided doses. There seems to be some reason to believe that a single dose at bedtime might work just as well. Within a few days, the dose will be raised to 150 mg a day. Raising the dose even higher becomes a matter of clinical judgement. The doctor must balance the side effects with the hoped for therapeutic effects. In some cases, doctors raise the dose of tricyclic medication to 200 or 300 mg per day. Protriptyline, another antidepressant, is somewhat energizing and the dose of that drug is considerably lower. Usually the total amount is 15 to 40 mg a day in three to four doses, this may be increased to 60 mg a day.

As has been noted in the section under clinical laboratory, people tend to metabolize or utilize drugs in different fashions. Should an individual receive what is considered to be an adequate dose of the medicine but not respond, it would be wise to obtain a blood level. It may be that adequate doses for one person are not adequate for another person. Thus, a person may be getting a dose of 150 or 200 mg a day of amitriptyline or imipramine but still not have an adequate level for therapeutic response. The determination of blood levels in the laboratory help determine whether this is the case.

What are side effects? They are rather similar for all of the tricyclic antidepressant drugs. Some are more or less likely to create a specific side effect because of their pharmaceutical action, but they have marked similarities. In the unusual case, confusional states with disorientation will occur with the tricyclic drugs. Withdrawal of the medicine is usually accompanied by a clearing of these symptoms. Lowered blood pressure and heart arrthymias may be seen with some of the drugs. This is a matter of some concern in the older patient who may be either hypertensive or have cardiac problems. It is not an absolute contraindication, but it is something that must be considered. Hypotension (low blood pressure) presents an interesting problem. Glassman and his colleagues have shown that hypotension is a significant problem with some of the tricyclic medications. This causes fainting and occasionally the person on tricyclics will fall and sustain a fracture. It is interesting that mental hospital data from Scandinavia show, in recent years, more accidents and fractures leading to death among hospitalized patients. This might be due to the increased use of drugs to treat depression, drugs which would cause lowered blood pressure and falling. Older patients with fragile bones would be especially at risk for problems of this kind.

Dry mouth, inability to urinate, and constipation are common side effects of the tricyclics. Some are more potent in causing these side-effects than others. Occasionally a person will develop a skin rash and on very rare occasions a person might develop some blood abnormality. Dizziness and fogginess are common in the beginning of treatment with tricyclics. Frequently this clears up as time goes on. On rare occasions jaundice will develop. This normalizes on withdrawal of the medicine. Abrupt withdrawal of tricyclic medication might produce some nausea and headache and a non-specific feeling of illness. In general, the common side-effects are not very serious. They include the minor ones such as dry mouth and constipation, dizziness and fogginess. Clinical supervision is absolutely necessary when a patient is put on these drugs in order to pick up any of the more serious complications.

Do tricyclics relieve depression? The answer to that is yes. Though there is a common view that the tricyclics take about three weeks to exert their effect, good studies by Braithewaite and Biggs and Ziegler show that improvement occurs within a week of therapy and that the rate of improvement is most marked within one to two weeks although it continues thereafter. There have been a number of other well-controlled studies. One of the best of these was that done by the British Medical Research Council where 72 per cent of patients treated with imipramine improved as against only 45 per cent of those treated with an inert drug (a placebo). When measuring a marked improvement, there was an advantage for the tricyclic of 52 per cent versus 39 per cent for the placebo, not as striking a difference. A study done over a ten-year period in Iowa revealed that 89 per cent of patients treated with an adequate dosage of tricyclics improved as opposed to only 60 per cent of those who had simple ward management or some kind of non-specific psychotherapy. However, marked improvement was the same for both groups, 26 per cent for the entire adequately treated tricyclic group versus 25 per cent for the ward milieu and non-specific psychotherapy group. 'Adequate' was defined as drug treatment for at least one month with the dose of tricyclics being 150 mg or more for at least two weeks. This is the treatment regimen used in the early studies showing that the drugs were effective. That the tricyclics are effective in helping patients with depression is clear. There is some question as to whether they work by suppressing some of the symptoms and giving the person an opportunity for a natural marked improvement to occur.

It has been noted that mood illness is associated with a higher mortality rate than would be expected in a normal population. Though there are relatively few studies which compare mortality in depressives treated with antidepressants versus those not so treated, what material there is on the subject suggests that adequate treatment with tricyclic medicine is associated with decreased mortality of depressive patients between discharge and one to three years.

In general, it has been noted that treatment with tricyclic antidepressants is more effective in those patients who are considered endogenous. This has suggested that tricyclic medication is getting at the heart of the matter, i.e. it is reversing the biological abnormality in depression. Indeed, these drugs should specifically deal with the biochemical abnormalities which have been implicated in mood illness. Tricyclic medication also manifests itself in a rather unusual way, which supports the previous statement. There seems some evidence now that certain predisposed patients who are treated with tricyclic medication will develop manias. Presumably, this would occur in individuals who had bipolar illness or at least a propensity for bipolar illness when they were treated for their depressions with tricyclic medication. More of these patients would develop a mania than would be expected by chance. This rather unusual side effect, i.e. the production of a manic episode in an individual so predisposed in a sense indicates the potent effect of the tricyclics on the basic biological background of the depressed patient.

One of the most important questions is whether the tricyclics can be used for prophylactic purposes. It is possible that tricyclic medication given to an individual who has had a depression and recovered will prevent subsequent episodes if the patient continues to take the medication. Common sense would indicate that this should occur if the tricyclics are to be considered effective.

In fact, there have been a number of studies on the effectiveness of tricyclic drugs in preventing relapse. Prien and his associates compared imipramine versus placebo in acute depressive illness. They found that 92 per cent of the placebo patients relapsed in the period of the study and only 63 per cent of the patients who were on imipramine. In England, Mindham and his co-investigators compared placebo with imipramine or amitriptyline. In eight months there was a striking difference between the two groups. Fifty per cent of the placebo group relapsed whereas only 22 per cent of the group treated with the tricyclics did so. Klerman and his associates in the Boston–New Haven study reported on a large number of patients who had initially been treated with amitriptyline. In those patients who had improved with treatment, they blindly put one group on amitriptyline for purposes of prevention and another group on placebo pills. The third group was put on no pills at all. When the investigators compared the active drug group, amitriptyline, with those who were on no active medicine, there was a striking difference. Forty per cent of the group treated with no active drug relapsed whereas only 15 per cent of the group treated with amitriptyline did so. Thus, the drug prevented the return of the symptoms. Similar findings were reported by Kay and his associates and also by Seager and Bird. In both of those studies, the active tricyclic did far better than the placebo. In the Kay study the placebo that was used was diazepam which is a drug used in treating the symptoms of anxiety. In this study, the diazepam patients relapsed in 47 per cent of the cases, the amitriptyline patients only in 24 per cent of the cases. To summarize, we are dealing with five separate studies, all of which report findings exactly in the same direction. Tricyclic medication prevents relapses in patients who have had a depressive illness. Davis calculated the probability that these prophylactic effects could have occurred by chance alone. He concluded that the probability that the findings were invalid and could have occurred simply by chance was 1.6 out of 100 000 000. Small chance indeed.

The findings on prevention of relapse tell us an important thing. Patients should be kept on tricyclic medication after improvement for some time, perhaps for as long as six to eight months. Also, in a person who is subject to multiple episodes of depression, it might be wise to consider using tricyclic medication over an indefinite period.

A second class of antidepressant drugs are the monoamine oxidase inhibitors. Monoamine oxidase inhibitors are usually not the physician's first choice for the treatment of a depressed patient. This is because of some potentially serious side-effects. Also, the tricyclics have seemed more effective in comparison trials. However, if a patient fails to respond to the tricyclic antidepressants, it is very reasonable to try one of the monoamine oxidase inhibitors (MAOIs). There are three of them that are in active use, isocarboxazid, phenelzine, and tranylcypromine. Of these three MAO inhibitors, phenelzine, is the one which has been studied most extensively.

Like the tricyclics, the monoamine oxidase inhibitors are associated with a biochemical rationale. This is directly related to the biogenic amine hypothesis. The biogenic amines noreprinephrine and serotonin are rendered pharmacologically inactive by an enzyme, monoamine oxidase. The monoamine oxidase inhibitors prevent the enzyme from working, thus increasing the amount of norepinephrine and serotonin in the brain, a desired effect in light of the biogenic amine hypothesis.

The question of efficacy in the monoamine oxidase inhibitors is a complicated one. The British National Research Council study found that such drugs were not more effective than placebo, but other studies have shown that they are useful. Klein and his collaborators have indicated that monoamine oxidase inhibitors may be particularly useful for depressed patients who are somewhat atypical. These might be patients who lack the symptoms of early morning awakening and appetite loss, but who are chronically unhappy and who may have too much sleep and are eating too much rather than too little. Certainly, clinicians have noted that patients who fail to respond to tricyclics may, on occasion, respond to the monoamine oxidase inhibitors. It is not unknown for an individual to be treated with a variety of tricyclics, fail to have any improvement, and finally in desperation to be placed on a monoamine oxidase inhibitor from which improvement may be rapid and marked. If an individual is to be switched from a tricyclic to a monoamine oxidase inhibitor, the first drug should be stopped and there should be a ten-day to two-week wait before changing to the monoamine oxidase inhibitor. The reason for this is that hypertensive crises sometimes occur when both drugs are given together. Nevertheless, tricyclics and monoamine oxidase inhibitors have been used together on therapy-resistant patients with no serious adverse effect. Countless cases of the concomitant use of the two drugs have been reported. There are no data, however, to indicate that the two drugs used together are more effective than either one alone. Himmelhoch and Detre and their co-workers have presented some evidence that suggests monoamine oxidase inhibtors, rather than tricyclics, may be the drugs of choice in depression occurring in bipolar patients.

Phenelzine is started by giving one 15 mg tablet on the first day. For the next three days, the person is given 30 mg a day. The dose is then raised to 30 mg twice a day or 60 mg a day. If no improvement occurs in four weeks, the dose may be raised as high as 90 mg for a period of a couple of weeks. Continuing lack of improvement would indicate that the drug should be stopped. Again, it should be noted that if the individual is to be changed to a tricyclic about two weeks of no medication should intervene before the change in medication.

There are some side effects that should be noted. These include low blood pressure, loss of appetite, and insomnia. Side-effects of this kind may require a dosage reduction. The major problem with the MAO inhibitors is a hypertension (raised blood pressure) which is caused by an interaction with certain foods or drugs. This interaction occurs because of the presence of tyramine which is found in some foods and beverages. Tyramine is ingested in an ordinary diet and is inactivated by the monoamine oxidase enzyme in the gastrointestinal tract and liver. If it is not inactivated, which could happen when given monoamine oxidase inhibitors, palpitations, severe headaches, and high blood pressure can result. There is a variety of foods and beverages which contain a great deal of tyramine and which might cause the unwanted side effects in the individuals taking monoamine oxidase inhibitors. These include various cheeses, pickled herring, fermented sausages and other fermented meats. Such alcoholic beverages as red wine and sherry should be avoided. In general, the patient who is put on a MAO inhibitor should be given a list of foods which he should avoid. Also, many drugs interact with MAO inhibitors and cause hypertension. These include stimulants, such as the amphetamines, some of the oral diabetic agents, Levodopa which is used to treat Parkinson's disease, and Demerol, a synthetic pain drug. Recently there have been findings which indicate that monoamine oxidase inhibitors might be useful in treating patients suffering from severe anxiousness and phobias. These are patients who ordinarily have secondary depressions and consequently monoamine oxidase inhibitors might be very useful for the treatment of secondary depressions.

The use of lithium in the treatment and prevention of manias and depressions is, all things considered, a real Cinderella story. Lithium is a naturally occurring substance which is in the same chemical group as sodium and potassium. Ordinarily lithium is administered as a salt, lithium carbonate. Cade introduced the use of lithium for manias in 1949. He noted that lithium produced a sedative-like action when administered to guinea pigs, and this gave him the idea that it might be useful in mania. In Europe, it was extensively studied and used. Schou made major contributions to understanding its clinical effects as well as the biochemistry of the lithium ion in the body. Because lithium was used as a salt substitute in the late 1940s in the United States with tragic consequences, death through toxicity, it took a long time before it was appreciated in the Western Hemisphere. In 1960 Gershon presented a clinical paper which helped interest American psychiatrists in the use of lithium.

If the body contains too much lithium, it produces significant toxic effects. In uncontrolled administration with high blood levels, one may find diarrhoea, weight loss, tremors, slurred speech, dizziness, convulsions, confusion, restlessness, stupor, coma, heart changes, circulatory collapse and ultimately, death. The secret to using lithium turned out to be rather simple. It was necessary to learn how to control the blood level. This can be done by using an uncomplicated flame photometer in the clinical laboratory.

Lithium is usually given as a carbonate in tablets or capsules which contain about 300 mg of lithium carbonate apiece. An individual will ordinarily take around three to six of these tablets or capsules over the course of a day. When started on lithium, an individual's blood should be drawn within one or two days after beginning the treatment. For lithium therapy to be completely safe, it is necessary that the level of the lithium in the blood plasma be kept from rising too high or too fast. If this happens, the dose should be lowered. A reasonable therapeutic blood level for treatment of a mania as assessed in the clinical laboratory is around 0.9 to 1.4 mE/l. If the blood level is too low, the dosage of the lithium carbonate should be increased. What is most important is that lithium treatment requires good clinical care and attention to both the physical and mental state of the individual as well as a knowledge of the lithium level in the blood. Normals who have taken lithium feel lethargic; this is also a complaint from some patients. On rare occasions, there are patients who retain lithium. These are people who when given even small doses build up an enormous blood level, ultimately leading to toxicity. By making frequent tests of levels in the beginning of treatment, it is possible to identify these people and to keep them from going into a toxic state. Once the lithium is regulated, it is wise to monitor the patient at reasonably frequent intervals and to obtain an occasional blood level in order to have an idea of what is going on.

In recent years there has been a concern that lithium might cause kidney damage. As some people are on lithium for years for the prevention of episodes of mania and depression, a physician should monitor kidney function at regular intervals. Lower maintenance blood levels (as low as 0.5 to 0.7 mEq/l) than were previously thought necessary may be helpful in preventing episodes of illness.

Is lithium effective? The answer to that is a resounding yes. This can be best put as a proportion: lithium is to mood disorders as antibiotics are to infectious diseases. In England, Coppen treated a number of bipolar (manic–depressive) patients as well as unipolar depressive patients. The unipolar depressives had had many episodes, as had the bipolar patients. Lithium was extremely effective in preventing subsequent attacks of mania and depression in these subjects. In the United States, Fieve and Dunner investigated the prevention of attacks in 35 bipolar patients and 28 unipolar patients. They compared the effect of lithium to the effect of a placebo. Lithium reduced the number of episodes that occurred during a year and decreased hospitalizations. This occurred for both the bipolar patients and the unipolar patients. In the bipolar patients, prevention occurred with lithium for both the depressive and manic episodes. A large National Institute of Mental Health–Veterans Administration study in the United States showed the same thing, lithium was extremely effective in preventing episodes of illness in bipolar patients.

No drug in psychiatry has been better studied than lithium. Evaluations have been very sound methodologically and the results are unequivocal. What is most interesting, however, is that the results with lithium are strongest in terms of prevention. When it comes to the treatment of an acute episode, we are dealing with a somewhat different problem. Certainly one would expect lithium to have an effect in an acute mania, and it does. One may expect a positive effect in one to three weeks ordinarily. However, in those patients who are extremely overactive and uncontrollable, it is often necessary to either add one of the neuroleptic drugs (major tranquillizers) to the lithium or to treat the person solely with a neuroleptic drug. Thus, in extremely hyperactive patients, a neuroleptic, such as chlorpromazine or haloperidol, acts more rapidly in reducing hyperactivity and bringing the patient under control. Lithium by itself is effective in the moderately hyperactive patient but in the extremely hyperactive patient neuroleptic treatment is often necessary. While the neuroleptic drug will get the patient under control more rapidly, lithium is superior in normalizing the thinking and mood. In one study, lithium had a relatively slow onset of action, averaging about eight days, but chlorpromazine acted much more rapidly in terms of lowering the excessive manic overactivity. However, once the person is brought under control, it is the lithium which is ordinarily the useful drug in preventing subsequent episodes.

There have been a number of reports of the use of lithium in patients who have depression. Generally, depressed patients who have a family history of mania or who themselves have had a mania in the past are considered to be better prospects for treatment with lithium than are other kinds of depressed patients. A recent study of the antidepressant effect of lithium on depression was recently reported by Worrall and colleagues. This was a blind study and concerned 63 depressed female in-patients who were subject to recurrent episodes of depression and mania. At the end of three weeks, these investigators reported that lithium had produced a more uniform improvement in the depressions than did the tricyclic imipramine. These striking findings suggest that lithium might be a very useful drug in the treatment of depression. One would doubt that it would be a first-choice drug for the treatment of acute unipolar depression, but in the case of bipolar depression, one might well consider it as the treatment of choice.

To summarize the section on the drug treatments of depression and mania, we might say that there is a variety of very good possibilities which have been well evaluated and which have reached the status of standard treatments. Not every patient will respond to each of these treatments and it requires some clinical judgement to change from one to the other. Nevertheless, the chances that a person with a depression or mania will respond both during the acute episode and with prevention of subsequent episodes are very good, thus making the whole field of treatment of affective disorders an optimistic one.

Electroconvulsive therapy

Electroconvulsive therapy (ECT) is the oldest effective treatment used for severe manias and depressions. It was introduced over 40 years ago by the Italians, Cerletti and Bini. In its early form, electrodes were placed on each temple and a current was passed between them. The patient had a *grand mal* convulsion which appeared similar to any epileptic seizure; the patient stiffened, and then had a series of jerkings in all the extremities. Witnesses considered it unpleasant to watch. It was associated with some fractures, particularly those of the vertebrae, and considerable forgetfulness occurred for a short time. For example, in the early days of ECT, a woman would be discharged home, vastly improved from her depression, but with a memory loss for a number of common details. Thus, upon arrival home she might ask her husband where the salt-pot was kept because she could not remember this simple item. Of interest is the fact that on relearning the location of the salt-pot, she retained this information. It took a couple of weeks for the patient to reorient herself. Times have changed considerably.

Currently, ECT is administered in the following fashion. A patient is scheduled to begin a series of ECT treatments. These are usually given three times a week on alternate days. On the night before a treatment, the patient is given nothing by mouth. This is to prevent the possibility of vomiting food at the time the treatment is given. About 30 minutes before the treatment, the patient is given a drug called atropine which dries up secretions in the respiratory tract. The patient is placed lying down on the treatment table. Dentures, glass eyes, contact lenses, hairgrips, combs, etc., are removed. A rubber mouthpiece is inserted in order to facilitate a good airway. The patient is given oxygen from a face-mask which is placed over the nose. Electrodes are placed on the patient's temples after electrode jelly has been rubbed into the skin in order to facilitate electrical contact. The physician inserts a needle into the patient's vein and injects a short-acting anaesthetic, methohexital, through the needle until the patient is asleep. Through the same needle, another drug, succinylcholine, is injected. Succinylcholine is a muscle relaxant. In about 45 to 60 seconds a current of desired voltage and time is administered. The patient then has a modified convulsion which manifests itself by a very light fluttering of the limbs or the muscles around the face. Thus, the treatment is given in such a way as to lighten the convulsion. The individual's anxiety is prevented by the anaesthesia and succinylcholine prevents the vigorous muscle jerkings. Because the movements are so light, no fractures of the vertebrae occur. Following this modified convulsion, the face-mask is placed over the patient's face and oxygen is released. Some physicians ventilate with oxygen producing artificial respiration until the patient starts to breathe on his own. The patient usually begins breathing spontaneously within 50 to 80 seconds after the end of the convulsion. Sometimes, on rare occasions, laryngeal spasm occurs and the patient has difficulty breathing. This can be dealt with by forcing the oxygen through the face mask. Delayed breathing has sometimes occurred because of inability to metabolize the succinylcholine; this occurs in patients with abnormal enzyme systems for the metabolism and breakdown of succinylcholine. Under these circumstances, artificial respiration will need to be continued for a prolonged period of time. However, this need not create any major problems. Ordinarily, after the treatment, the patient rests for a while and then eats breakfast.

Patients with unusual or severe cardiac, respiratory, or

skeletal diseases are considered at high risk, but these do not necessarily have to be considered as contraindications for the treatment. Age is no contraindication. Patients at 80 have been given ECT with no difficulty. Pregnancy is not a contraindication. Indeed, ECT may be the safest treatment of any for episodes of mood disorder. Given bilaterally (the current between the temples) confusion and memory loss still occur. It is now possible to give the treatments unilaterally. Thus, both electrodes are placed on one side of the head rather than on opposite sides of the head. In this kind of treatment, there is less confusion and memory loss. In fact, it is often difficult to determine any significant confusion. In some hospitals, all treatment is given unilaterally in order to prevent confusion. In other hospitals, physicians believe that the bilateral treatment is slightly more effective than the unilateral treatment and prefer the former.

The one specific contraindication to ECT being given for depression or mania is the presence of a brain tumour. Maltbie and his co-workers evaluated the risk of ECT in patients who had brain tumours. They found that most patients demonstrated a mental or physical deterioration, or both, following ECT. It seems clear that a known brain tumour should certainly be a contraindication for ECT.

Although ECT has been around for 40 years, the exact mechanism by which it exerts its influence is unknown. There is a general consensus that the therapeutic effect is dependent on producing a convulsion. Though this convulsion may be modified completely and be almost unrecognizeable because of anaesthesia and muscle relaxants (succinylcholine), the electrical current still causes the common kinds of brain wave changes that one sees with a convulsion.

Cronholm and Ottosson in Sweden altered the induction of the convulsion and noted that the electrical current itself was not necessarily relevant but rather the convulsion itself. An interesting study was reported by Freeman and his co-workers. They gave two real ECTs to patients and to another group they gave two 'pseudo-ECTs'. After the *bona fide* and simulated ECTs, all patients received real ECT. The group treated with the real ECT showed significantly more improvement than the group that were treated with the sham therapy. Ulett and his co-workers induced convulsions by photostimulation. This appeared to be equally as successful in treating depression as ECT itself. Thus, the induction of the convulsion seems to be the common denominator for the mechanism of action. Further work, however, has to be done on this particular problem. Some animal experiments suggest that ECT influences the biogenic amines and their receptors thus indicating a possible neurochemical rationale for the treatment.

Testing memory impairment with ECT is complicated by the fact that depressives frequently do rather badly on intellectual tasks because of the illness. Sometimes they show cognitive impairment in these tests, and after ECT this difficulty in thinking clears up and the patients do better. Nevertheless, there may be some memory loss associated with ECT. Patients often complain of loss of memory for events occurring around the time of the treatments and this loss persists. This question is not totally answered as yet. Squire gave a battery of memory tests to patients who had received both bilateral and unilateral ECT for depression six to nine months before taking the tests. There was no evidence of any specific learning deficits which might be caused by the ECT. Most studies show that no important intellectual deficits are associated with ECT.

The important question has to do with the effectiveness of ECT in the treatment of depression. There is nothing more striking in psychiatry than the very retarded, acutely depressed patient who after two or three ECTs normalizes and is able to function. Patients who have acute depressions, who do not have marked personality problems, and who have typical depressive symptoms seem to be the best candidates for ECT. Wechsler reviewed over 150 studies which involved a total of almost 6000 patients. Average improvement in these studies occurred in about 72 per cent of patients treated with ECT. However, in treating chronic depressions, only 37 per cent of patients responded to the ECT.

Management and specific treatment

ECT, though it looks very specific, is really not. McCabe has shown good evidence of its efficacy in treating acute mania. In fact, there may be cases when manic patients are more effectively treated with ECT than they are with the major tranquillizing (neuroleptic) drugs. Also ECT has been used to terminate occasional deliria that occur because of known organic causes. However, it is in the treatment of depression that ECT has been most frequently used and is considered the most useful. Many studies comparing ECT with other treatments of depression, namely monoamine oxidase inhibitors and tricyclic antidepressants, show that ECT is the most effective treatment. Avery and Winokur presented comparisons of various kinds of treatment in hospitalized depressed patients who entered the hospital over a period of ten years, 1959–1969. There were 519 depressed patients in the group that was studied. Patients were followed up for periods of one and three years and it was noteworthy that patients treated with electroconvulsive therapy had a lower mortality rate in the follow-up period than those patients who received no drug treatment or inadequate drug treatment. If one examined adequate drug treatment and electroconvulsive therapy, there was a striking decrease in mortality in both of these groups as opposed to the patients who were treated with inadequate doses of medicine or ward management or non-specific psychological management. In particular heart attacks were considerably fewer in the group that were offered adequate treatment (adequate drug treatment or ECT-adequate treatment). Increased mortality was a particularly large problem in those patients 50 years and older who received inadequate treatment. In the late 1940s, Huston made the important discovery that ECT prevented both mortality and suicide in depressed patients when compared to untreated depressed control patients. In the study of 519 depressed patients, there were 609 hospitalizations. Efficacy was compared in a variety of groups (Fig. 12.1). ECT and antidepressant therapy both produced improvement in patients with depression. However, if one simply looked at marked improvement, an interesting

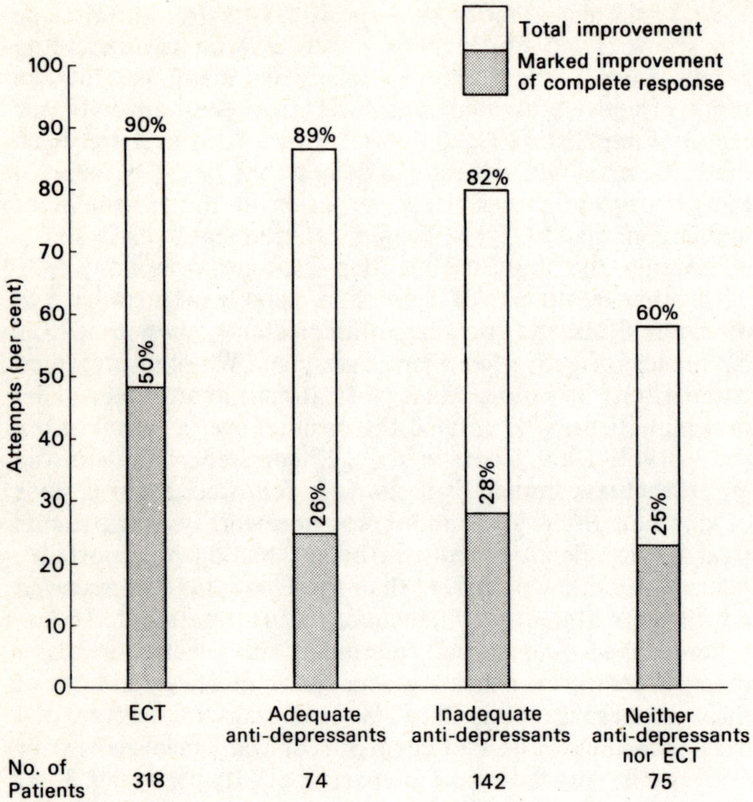

Fig. 12.1. Improvement and marked improvement in differently treated hospitalized depressives. (Based on data from D. Avery and G. Winokur *Biological psychiatry* (1977).)

finding emerged. ECT was twice as likely to be associated with marked improvement as either adequate antidepressant therapy, inadequate antidepressant therapy, or neither ECT nor antidepressant therapy (ward management or non-specific psychotherapy). Thus, it seems clear that ECT is far more likely to create a marked improvement or a remission to the previous well state than any other treatment which we now have. It made no difference whether the person was unipolar or bipolar, old or young, male or female. ECT was the more effective treatment in creating a marked improvement. Specific symptoms seem to make no difference. ECT was still superior. This study dealt with clinical experience, but the fact happens to be that similar findings on 'marked improvement' occurred in Greenblatt's study in Boston. Only ECT created a significant increase in marked improvement. Neither placebo nor treatment with a tricyclic antidepressant was able to approach this amount of marked improvement.

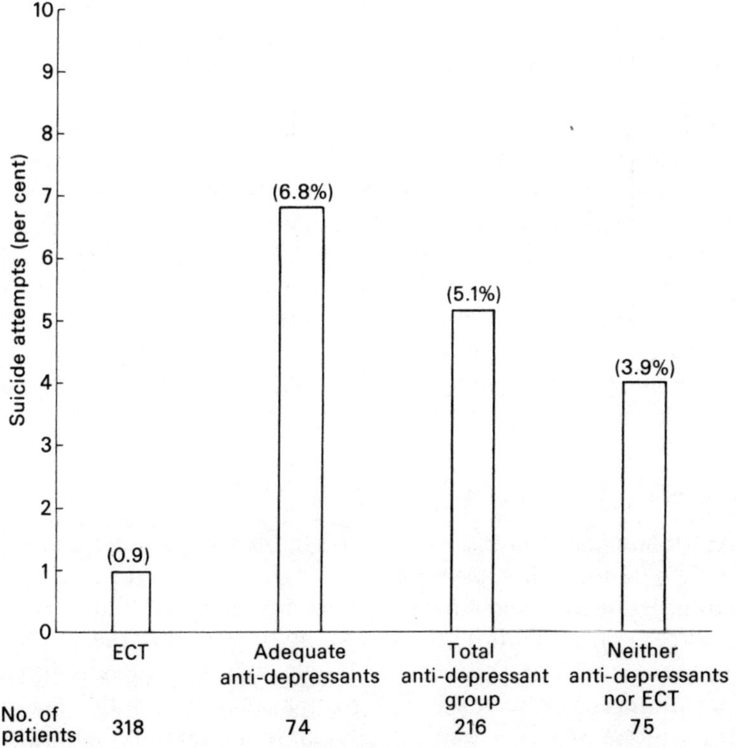

Fig. 12.2. Suicide attempts after admission and at 6-month follow-up in differently treated groups of hospitalized depressives. (Based on data from D. Avery and G. Winokur *Archives of General Psychiatry* (1978).)

Suicide and attempted suicide during hospitalization and in the six months after discharge were compared to the treatment groups in the 519 patients. Figure 12.2 presents this material. What seems clear is that the ECT group was associated with fewer suicide attempts than any of the other groups.

The real question about ECT is whether it is effective. That seems to have been proved. The next question is should it ever be the treatment of choice in a depressed person. As it appears to be more effective in producing a marked improvement, one could make the case that in a person who is at a high risk for suicide, ECT should be the treatment of choice. Thus a hospitalized depressive who was male, middle-aged, and intent on doing away with himself might very well be the kind of patient in whom ECT would be the first treatment considered.

ECT is probably used less frequently than required. In a 10-year span at a mid-western United States hospital, ECT use dropped from 60 per cent of the eligible depressives to 20 per cent. The use of antidepressants rose from 20 per cent to 60 per cent. This occurred in spite of the fact that the psychiatrists in the hospital were signing out the ECT patients as more likely to have improved. Obviously clinical behaviour in this case is motivated by something besides science.

Specific psychotherapy

As depression bears a passing resemblance to unhappiness, the possibility that psychotherapy might be useful in alleviating depression immediately comes to mind. After all, better interpersonal functioning should help clear up the dreary effects of unpleasant situations. Psychotherapy or counselling, or whatever one wants to call it, is a treatment which spans the professions. Not only do psychiatrists have an interest in it but also psychologists, social workers, and counsellors. For economic purposes, the most prevalent and least expensive psychotherapist might well be the social worker. Before concerning ourselves with who might do the psychotherapy, however, it is necessary to determine whether it is of any value.

Weissmann, Prusoff, and their co-workers have published extensively on the effect of interpersonal psychotherapy as a treatment for depression. Interpersonal psychotherapy is a treatment which goes on the assumption that depression develops in a social context and that the development is determined by significant interpersonal relationships between the depressed person and other people. Interpersonal psychotherapy is offered in an attempt to improve symptoms and social adjustment. No claim is made that it has an impact on permanent personality difficulties. Psychotherapists attempt to improve the patient's social functioning by increasing his ability to deal with external stresses and by helping the patient manage the personal and social consequences of the disorder. Within the context of interpersonal psychotherapy, specific techniques have been developed for managing depressed patients with grief and loss, interpersonal deficits, and marital problems. There has been a recent attempt to determine its efficacy. Four groups were evaluated. One group obtained amitriptyline, another group obtained individual interpersonal psychotherapy, a third group obtained both the drug and the psychotherapy, and a fourth group consisted of patients who were offered supportive psychotherapy on demand. As regards symptom reduction, both amitriptyline and psychotherapy were about equally effective, but the drug in combination with such psychotherapy resulted in additional symptom reduction. In other words, both treatments used together seem to be more effective than either one alone. The antidepressant mainly improved such symptoms as sleep and appetite disturbances whereas psychotherapy mainly affected mood, suicidal ideation, work, and interests. The group that was treated with supportive therapy on demand did worse than any other group. In general, the patients were not severely depressed and all were treated as out-patients. The study suggests that psychotherapy is useful in the treatment of depression, but there is one caveat. The same group was involved in the Boston–New Haven study which was described above in the section on drug treatment. In that study, 150 recovering depressed women were placed in two groups. One group received interpersonal psychotherapy; the other did not. Amitriptyline was given to some of the patients in each of these two groups. There was a marked difference in response. The group receiving psychotherapy had improved social and interpersonal function. However, only the use of an antidepressant prevented relapse and the return of symptoms. Certainly, these two studies differed. In one the patients were treated and then put on maintenance therapy, whereas in the other the patients were treated initially with psychotherapy or drugs or both or support on demand. Nevertheless, one could reasonably assume if psychotherapy were particularly effective it should have manifested itself in prevention of relapse (the development of symptoms) in the maintenance treatment study.

Some explanation may be noted in recent work by this group. Those patients with a situational depression (similar to non-endogenous, neurotic–reactive depression) responded to interpersonal psychotherapy or tricyclic medication alone. However, those patients with an endogenous depression did not respond to interpersonal psychotherapy alone. Thus, having an endogenous depression predicted a poor response in the interpersonal psychotherapy group, but it did predict a good response if drug treatment were added to the interpersonal psychotherapy. Actually these findings make sense if one considers the definitions. Endogenous depression is presumably a depression that comes from within the body whereas situational depression is presumably a response to psychosocial circumstances without. Psychological treatment in the situational group would be a rational treatment; but in the endogenous group it does not appear to be the treatment of choice.

A second approach to the psychotherapy of depression is behaviour therapy, where the treatment is based on the idea that the depression is related to behaviours which elicit few positive reinforcements from the environment. Patients are taught to engage in behaviour which will obtain rewarding experiences for them. Lewinsohn has reported some success with behaviour therapy but more trials are necessary to determine the efficacy in this type of treatment as compared to drugs. Also, it is necessary to know if the treatment will be useful in patients as severely affected as those seen in a psychiatric clinic.

Another important psychotherapy used for the treatment of depression has been called cognitive therapy. It has been investigated extensively by Beck and Rush and their collaborators. It is based on the idea that the depressed person tends to regard himself and his future in a very negative fashion. This, of course, is true. Self-condemnation and self-abnegation, as well as feelings of worthlessness, are common in depressed patients. Cognitive therapy is offered to correct negative concepts, which in turn should alleviate depressive symptoms. A study of 41 unipolar depressed out-patients were either treated with cognitive therapy or imipramine. The cognitive therapist attempts to use both verbal and behavioural techniques to help the patient recognize connections between cognition, feeling states, and behaviour. Also the cognitive therapist attempts to get the patient to learn to monitor his negative thoughts and to examine evidence for and against his abnormal ideas about himself. Finally, the cognitive therapist attempts to substitute more reality-oriented interpretations for the patient's distorted self-condemnatory feelings. Presumably the patient is to learn to identify and alter beliefs which he has been distorting. In this study cognitive therapy resulted in a much greater improvement than imipramine treatment. Almost 80 per cent of the patients in cognitive therapy showed a marked improvement or a complete remission of symptoms as compared to less than a quarter of the imipramine patients. Short-term follow-up indicated that the gains were maintained over time. What makes the study even more striking is the fact that the patients had been either intermittently or chronically depressed for a number of years, since the first onset of depression, and 75 per cent of them were suicidal. There is no doubt that this is a very positive study in favour of the use of psychotherapy for depression. Again, the patients are out-patients rather than hospitalized patients and one must question whether similar results would be found in acutely depressed patients who need to be hospitalized. In fact, the results of this study are relevant to the next section of this chapter, namely the treatment of therapy-resistant patients. It would appear from the description of the patients in the cognitive therapy study that they were chronic, ruminative patients who had been ill off an on for a long period of time and had not been good responders in the past. It would be interesting if this were exactly the kind of patient in which cognitive therapy were particularly effective.

The therapy-resistant patient

Ten to twenty-five per cent of depressed patients run a chronic course. More bipolar patients may have this kind of development than unipolar patients. In spite of vigorous treatment, a certain number of patients simply do not get well. Years ago before the development of ECT, a middle-aged patient might enter the hospital and stay there for 8 to 10 years in the throes of a retarded and unremitting depression. At the end of this time, the patient might begin to improve and ultimately be discharged. Such a patient would return home and take up where he or she left off in the past. Thus, chronicity, though it may last a long time, was not necessarily permanent. Development of effective treatment made a difference for the vast majority of patients but even today some patients remain resistant to any kind of therapy. When a psychiatrist encounters a therapy-resistant patient, he must use his imagination to develop a therapeutic regimen. We have already noted that cognitive therapy may be of use in the therapy-resistant patient. Likewise, there are a variety of other possibilities. The addition of thyroid hormone to ordinary antidepressant treatment sometimes produces a result. In a few cases, it has been reported that adrenal cortex hormones may make some positive difference. Clinical observations have indicated that an elderly patient with depression who has considerable diurnal variation may be helped over a rough spot in the day by a small dose of an amphetamine (such as methylamphetamine, 5–10 mg in the morning). Just as a note, few elderly patients who have shown lifelong stability are likely to become addicted to the medication.

Many of the chronic patients these days are able to function in the outside world but still have some symptoms. Some, however, are not able to function outside hospital and these must be considered to be the most serious cases. It is in these cases that one may consider a more radical type of treatment, psychosurgery. Ballantine and his co-workers in Boston reported on 154 psychiatric patients who underwent an operation entitled bilateral anterior stereotatic cingulotomy. Unrelenting depression was the most frequent symptom in the group, and they reported that mood disorders were most often improved postoperatively.

Mitchell-Heggs and co-workers in England reported on an operation called a stereotactic limbic leucotomy. In a small series of depressive patients, 78 per cent of patients were considered improved at 16 months. They also reported that adverse effects from the treatment had not been a problem following this operation. Newer psychosurgical methods have been associated with less morbidity than the older, more extensive operations. The newer operations tend to involve very small areas of brain tissue. There are fewer cognitive disturbances and fewer problems with neurological symptoms such as convulsion. In fact, with the operations such as those described above, it is not possible for the casual observer to tell that the person has had an operation. The patients act in an ordinary fashion.

There is one huge advantage that depressed patients have as regards psychosurgery. Ordinarily, depressed patients are totally competent mentally and able to make decisions. Thus, they may be presented with the situation and asked to give an informed consent. If they suffer enough from the symptoms of depression, it is quite possible that they will agree to the operation because the prospects of the alleviation of the symptoms are enticing. Should the patient say that he is opposed to the operation, it is highly unlikely that the operation would be done in these times.

Almost monthly new possibilities for treating therapy-resistant patients arise. New antidepressants are constantly being tested and marketed. Perhaps some of these will have some special effect. Because of the fact that some antidepressants prevent reuptake of serotonin and others prevent the reuptake of norepinephrine, it is possible that switching from one antidepressant to another could be of some use. Other aspects of the biogenic amine hypothesis have been used to initiate new treatments. A good example of this is found in a report of treatment of 99 out-patients with therapy-resistant depressions. Van Hiele in the Netherlands treated these patients with L–5-hydroxytrytophan, which is a metabolic product of tryptophan and ultimately is converted to serotonin. The idea is that administration of L–5-hydroxytryptophan would increase the amount of serotonin in the brain and thereby relieve the depression. One can see that this treatment is based on one of the accepted theoretical possibilities for the cause of depression. The author reports that recovery occurred without side effects in 50 per cent of these therapy-resistant patients. As a matter of fact, there have been numerous studies of the effects of tryptophan and L-tryptophan in the treatment of depression. A conservative estimate of its usefulness is that it may have some antidepressant effects in some depressed patients. Further, L-tryptophan may increase the antidepressant activity of monoamine oxidase inhibitors. However, this point has not been proved beyond a shadow of a doubt. A clinical example of this kind of thinking may be useful at this juncture.

Mr N. S. was a 41-year-old, married, unemployed, research assistant from a state biological laboratory. He had a 17-year history of recurrent depressive episodes. He had had multiple hospitalizations during which he had been treated with tricyclic antidepressants, monoamine oxidase inhibitor antidepressants, a combination of the two, lithium and ECT. None led to complete remission although during periods of particularly deep depression ECT was effective in bringing him back to his usual status. There was a question of whether he had ever had mania as he had had several brief episodes of hypomanic behaviour but never one which was clear-cut. Because he had been so ruminative for years and because he was so unsure of himself and compulsive in his behaviour, he was not able to perform any work and had been sacked from his job five years before the present admission. His sacking was due to 'slowness and inefficiency at work'. Even when he was well, however, he was very ruminative and slow. At the time of admission, he had been on a downhill slide for several weeks. He had serious doubts about self-worth. He was hopeless about ever being well. He could not concentrate. He had no energy and he lacked interest. He was unable to make a decision, had no sexual drive, and had a loss of appetite. He appeared markedly slowed up in both his speech and activities.

A conference was held to determine whether after 17 years, psychosurgery ought to be considered in this patient. The patient had been at his wits end and was in favour of surgery if the physicians could offer any hope that it would be useful. It was agreed among the hospital staff that he was a legitimate candidate for psychosurgery, but first it was decided to try two novel medical approaches. The first of these was to load his diet with glutamate together with low-dose isoniazide as a precursor loading strategy to increase gamma-aminobutyric acid. The second suggestion was to treat him with tryptophan in addition to a monoamine oxidase inhibitor in order to increase the level of available serotonin. He was started on the glutumate loading the day after the staffing. After ten days this was discontinued with no improvement. He was then started on the monoamine inhibitor and the tryptophan. The patient bought the tryptophan at a health foods store because it was not available in the hospital pharmacy. He was given 3 g per day of L-tryptophan and 15 mg four times a day of phenelzine, a monoamine oxidase inhibitor. After he had been on this for several days, he remarked to his doctor in morning rounds that for the last 15 minutes he had been feeling considerably better than he had throughout all the rest of his hospitalization. This is the kind of acute response that is sometimes seen in patients, particularly those with bipolar illness. Independently, that afternoon, the nurses noted that he was more participant in activities, that he no longer seemed as retarded and that he was improving. He appeared motivated and responsive and interested in things. He had a more positive outlook about himself. The improvement seemed to occur in several days after starting him on the L-tryptophan. It is highly unlikely that the improvement was due to a placebo effect. Had it been, he should have responded to the first type of treatment, that with glutamate. On the other hand, the patient had had a number of spontaneous remissions in the past, and it is quite conceivable that his remission at this point with the tryptophan and the monoamine oxidase inhibitor was nothing more nor less than a spontaneous remission. In any case, he was discharged on the same regimen. Only a follow-up will determine if this regimen will be associated by any substantial improvement in the long run.

The above is a fairly good idea of the kind of imaginative treatment that might be used in the unusual patient. Post recently has shown some evidence that carbamazepine may be useful in treating mania. This drug presents a problem as it has been implicated in causing blood abnormalities. However, with careful monitoring of the blood, it may achieve some place in treating the therapy-resistant patient. Within the past few months a couple of psychiatrists have reported good results in treating a few depressed patients with L-tyrosine, a compound found in the diet. This supplementation of tyrosine in the diet, like the tryptophan supplementation, is rational treatment according to the current theories of depression. These days it appears that new treatment possibilities arise as frequently as the new moon. Certainly other treatments are possible and one should never feel hopeless in treating a patient with a potentially remitting disease. Probably the ambience of enthusiasm and the institution of imaginatively new therapeutic ideas is in itself helpful. Certainly, there are enough very plausible theories and findings at the present time to make a variety of different trials worth-while.

13

What the family should know

Old wives' tales concerning the subject of depression abound. We are told that depressed patients who become suicidal do not communicate their intent to anybody. That is certainly not true. We are told that the Christmas holidays increase the risk for depression. That is certainly not true either. We are told that depressives will ultimately become schizophrenics. That was a popular belief in the late 1940s even among distinguished psychiatrists. It is certainly not true. Some believe that all psychiatric illnesses are the same essentially, only differing in severity. Thus, all people are ill, the most seriously ill being psychotic, the less seriously being neurotic. Even the person with no diagnosis is ill, just not as severely. The implication is that all illnesses are caused by distressing life circumstances and the manifestations are not very important, only the circumstances. This kind of viewpoint is hardly supportable. However, most facts, particularly the genetic data, suggest we are dealing with a variety of specific illnesses.

In the face of a multitude of opinions, it is necessary to discuss what the family should know about depression and about the depressed patient.

In a sense the most important thing is that the family recognize the clinical picture of depression or mania. False perceptions may lead to serious consequences, consequences which can be prevented with appropriate recognition and treatment. It is important to note that most patients with mood disorders have remitting illnesses. Such patients will get well in time. They will not become grossly insane and relegated to a mental hospital for the rest of their lives.

The family should be aware of the fact that the most important thing in the beginning is to obtain a valid and reliable diagnosis on the patient. It is necessary to find a psychiatrist who is willing to put in some time examining the patient. If there is any question about the diagnosis, it is entirely reasonable that the family seek a second opinion. Once a diagnosis has been made, the family should expect the psychiatrist to take responsibility for prescribing the treatment and for managing the case. If this is not possible, it is his obligation to find an appropriate situation in which the patient can be adequately followed in a clinical fashion. It is not too much of the family to ask that the physician return reasonable telephone calls and be available when questions arise.

If the patient is in the hospital, the family will probably want to visit. There is no evidence that keeping the family and the patient apart under ordinary circumstances helps anything. Sometimes it does make it a little easier on the part of the hospital not to have the family around, but on the other hand it makes it a little harder on the part of the patient and the family not to see each other. If there are any restrictions on visiting, the family should attempt to find out in some depth why this is necessary. Years ago patients and families were separated for several weeks or months. The idea was that as the patient became ill in the context of the family interaction, separation would hasten improvement. Today, very few people would find this viewpoint valid.

If the patient is being treated as an out-patient, the family should not ask too much of him during the period of illness. On the other hand, the family should attempt to involve him in anything that he finds reasonable and pleasurable. Specifically the family should not request complicated intellectual tasks of the patient. Alternatively, to involve him in physical activities or sports seems appropriate, particularly if these cause no unusual objections on the patient's part.

It is very important that the family should not take the blame for the patient's illness. There is no reason to believe that anything the family did caused the illness. In any family, there are good times and bad times and no doubt the patient, like any ill person, will respond with irritability, unhappiness, or pleasure to changing circumstances. This is not necessarily very relevant to causing the illness. Often parents are concerned that they did something wrong, thus making their child depressed or manic. This is simple nonsense, and the family should recognize it.

One of the most important things to keep in mind is the question of taking responsibility for decisions. Several years ago a patient appeared in the office of a psychiatrist, after having been discharged from a mental hospital. He had been sent to the hospital after shooting himself in the mouth. As luck would have it, he missed every vital organ and lived to tell the tale.When he visited the office of the psychiatrist in the company of his wife, he was as depressed and self-condemnatory as when he had made the suicide attempt. The psychiatrist said that the patient needed to be in the hospital because he was a danger to himself. The wife did not feel she could take the responsibility for bringing the patient into hospital against his will. Because the patient had a depression from which he would ultimately recover, it seemed important to treat him. Certainly when he recovered, he would be sorry if he did anything to permanently injure himself. On some occasions the family has to take responsibility to do something against the patient's wishes. In modern times there are very responsible commitment laws to protect the patient against any familial or professional infringement of liberties. In the case of an individual who is very ill with a depression or mania, the family should recognize that on occasion they must take the responsibility for hospitalization. Often the patient will tell the family members that he will never forgive them. The family is then unwilling to make the decision. However, the question should be not whether he will ever forgive them but whether it is better that he should be alive under any circumstances. Possibly it is this last that is the appropriate question.

The family must recognize that often the patient will engage in behaviour which will create social problems. Often a manic patient will drink too much and even, on some occasions, a depressed patient will drink too much. This kind of secondary alcoholism is really part of the depression, and it is important that the patient receive treatment for the depression rather than be considered weak and unable to control himself.

One of the most interesting problems with which the family contends is what happens when they are confronted with a series of interpretations of behaviour. A husband was confronted with the following situation. He had gone out of town on a business trip. He had left his wife behind. She had suffered from an anxiety attack and visited a local psychiatrist. The local psychiatrist saw the patient, examined her, and told the husband that the patient had remarked on the fact that the psychiatrist had muddy shoes, and was not as professional appearing as he might be. The psychiatrist interpreted this as her showing good strength of character (ego strength). Therefore, he was not so terribly concerned about her psychiatric problems. Nevertheless, he asked that the woman visit a second time. The woman did visit the second time. At that time, she apologized for having remarked about the psychiatrist's shoes, feeling that she had been rude. The psychiatrist then told the husband that her personality was weaker than his first estimate. He suggested that she might decompensate and become more ill. Then, he recommended hospitalization to the husband. The husband accepted this. The patient spent a year in the hospital with a working diagnosis of schizophrenia. She was discharged with absolutely no change in her clinical picture from when she entered. She continued to have anxiety attacks, which she had before hospitalization. The idea of making a diagnosis on interpretation of motivation or behaviour is foolishness. The family should be very wary of it.

The family should recognize certain things about the onset. An acute onset of the illness is usually more likely seen in a mood disorder than it is in another psychotic illness, schizophrenia. If the individual becomes ill on the top of rather good social, marital, and job functioning, it is highly suggestive of a mood disorder. Thus, the illness is also highly likely to be remitting and have a good future. It is often important to recognize that absolute recovery may take some time.

Treatment may moderate the symptoms and send the patient back into the community or social circumstance from which he came. Nevertheless, he may continue to have lingering symptoms for a period of time. This should not discourage the family because these symptoms too will go in time.

Because the mood disorders are heavily familial and often genetic, one should consider the appropriateness of genetic counselling. Crowe cogently outlined six principles of genetic counselling which include the necessities of accurate diagnoses and accurate family histories. Also, there should be a good evaluation of the individual who is requesting counselling. With these beginnings, the counsellor may discuss the problems of risk (the probability that a child will be affected with the illness). He also must discuss the problem of burden which is concerned with the severity of the illness and the kinds of problem that this might create for an ill person and his family in society. The decision as to whether to have children is essentially in the hands of the patient, but it is necessary that he understand the circumstances. Finally, the genetic counsellor must satisfy himself that the person who he is counselling fully understands the discussion.

In the case of unipolar depression, the family should understand that more than one type of illness is encountered in that category. It is a heterogenous collection of illnesses. The risk of suffering from a mood illness in a first-degree relative of a depressed patient is between 9 and 14 per cent, females being at somewhat higher risk than males. First-degree relatives have about five times the risk for depression of the general population. The specific type of inheritance is unknown for any of the subgroups of unipolar depression. The person who is asking for counselling should understand the consequences of the illness and should be knowledgeable about the extensive possibilities for treatment.

In bipolar mood disorders, the picture is somewhat different. The first-degree relatives of bipolar patients have a higher risk for illness than first-degree relatives of unipolar patients. It is about 20 per cent. Considerable evidence indicates that there may be two types of transmission, one sex-linked and the other non-sex-linked. However, this is not accepted by all and certainly bipolar illness should not be presented as a sex-linked disorder. The reason for not presenting it as a sex-linked disorder is that the counselling could be in error if the family had a non-sex-linked type of bipolar illness. Most data indicate that the risk is higher in females than in males which would indicate the possibility that some part of bipolar illness may be sex-linked. People being counselled should understand that the illness is familial but that the exact type of inheritance is unknown. Also, they should understand the manifestations and consequences of the illness and the fact that a number of effective treatments are available for both the management of acute episodes as well as prevention of episodes.

Finally, the family should know something about where to seek their first contact if a matter of concern has arisen about a family member. There are a number of legitimate places. They include a local physician, a local hospital or clinic, a psychiatric clinic run by a department in the medical school, or any available physician. Medical students are taught about mood disorders during their schooling. Consequently, there should be plenty of professionals who are able to direct the family to where they can seek appropriate care.

Appendix 1

Criteria for diagnosing mania and depression (adapted from the *Diagnostic and statistical manual of mental disorders of the American Psychiatric Association, DSM-III* (3rd edition), with some minor changes and additions).

These criteria in essence are the ones which are used by psychiatrists for making a diagnosis of mania or depression.

I. Diagnostic criteria for mania

(a) A distinct period of an elevated, expansive, or irritable mood;
(b) duration of one week, at least;
(c) three or four of the following symptoms:
  (i) increase in activity (in social, work, or sexual situations);
  (ii) more talkative than usual, pressure to keep talking;
  (iii) racing thoughts or ideas brought forth at increased rate. each tumbling over the other;
  (iv) grandiosity (may or may not be delusional);
  (v) decreased sleep;
  (vi) distractibility, i.e. attention drawn to trivial external stimuli;
  (vii) excessive involvement in activities, e.g. buying sprees, sexual activity, social intrusiveness, foolish investments, reckless driving, unnecessary long distance telephone calls;
(d) must rule out
  (i) schizophrenia, schizophreniform disorder, paranoid disorder;
  (ii) possible organic causes of mania, such as am-

phetamines, steroids, multiple sclerosis, thyrotoxicosis, general paresis.

II. Diagnostic criteria for a primary major depression

(a) A distinct period of depressed, sad, hopeless, irritable, or low mood accompanied by a loss of interest or pleasure in usual activities;
(b) duration of at least two weeks;
(c) at least four of the following symptoms:
 (i) poor appetite or weight loss;
 (ii) sleeplessness or excessive sleeping;
 (iii) agitation or slowing down (retardation) of physical activity;
 (iv) loss of interest or pleasure in usual activities or decreased sexual drive;
 (v) loss of energy, fatigue;
 (vi) feelings of worthlessness, guilt, or self-condemnation (may or may not be delusional);
 (vii) complaints of inability to think or concentrate, or slowed thinking, marked indecisiveness;
 (viii) recurrent thoughts of death or suicide, or suicide attempt;
(d) Not superimposed on
 (i) schizophrenia, schizophreniform disorder, paranoid disorder, or any other psychiatric illness which precedes the depression (if superimposed, the depression is considered a 'secondary depression');
 (ii) organic mental disorder due to such causes as reserpine, influenza, hypothryroidism, a life-threatening disease, Alzheimer's disease, or other brain diseases leading to dementia;
 (iii) bereavement (death of close relative or friend).

Appendix 2

Medical students learn about medicine by seeing patients. There is no way to get a real feeling for the clinical picture without seeing a patient. The next best thing is to read a case history. It helps to make a written text about a particular illness come alive.

Following are several illustrative case reports of patients who have had depressions and manias. All of these patients were admitted to the Iowa Psychiatric Hospital over 40 years ago. All are deceased. To the clinical material, there has been a commentary added which emphasizes some of the important points and takes up some aspects of treatment.

Case 1: Mrs K. was a 53-year-old woman who was admitted because of the symptoms of agitation, restlessness, and ideas of self-depreciation, these symptoms being present for six months before admission.

Around six months before being admitted, the patient had become depressed, in the context of her husband losing considerable money. She began to sit around, cry, and to feel that she was a burden on the family. She had no hope. She lost 20 lb in weight, and she developed delusions (delusions are fixed false beliefs) about a growth in the nose and throat. She made two suicidal attempts. When seen in the hospital, she was agitated and talked in a hoarse croaking voice. She expressed many ideas of self-depreciation. Her intelligence quotient was average, 100.

She left the hospital after a month and a half, still ill. She was kept at home for a year and then taken to a private sanatorium where she remained for another year. She spent several years at two other private sanatoriums and finally was given five metrazol shock treatments (the precursor to electroshock therapy) which resulted in no improvement. So, except for one year at home she had been continuously in the hospital for a period of about seven years when she was readmitted again to the Iowa Psychiatric Hospital. The second admission to the original hospital was accomplished with the idea of seeing whether or not the patient who, by this time, was 60 years old would be a fit candidate for electroshock treatment. When admitted she was preoccupied and appeared bland and indifferent. Her memory and orientation were good but she had X-ray signs of brain atrophy, particularly in the parietal region.

On the basis of this abnormal laboratory finding, it was considered that the patient had some kind of organic brain disease and was never treated.

Comment: This is a patient with a fairly late onset depression and it is just this kind of patient who does extremely well with electroconvulsive therapy. Even in the face of the abnormal pneumoencephalogram (a type of X-ray examination), the patient was oriented and had no memory defect. It is quite possible that the abnormal X-ray findings were not relevant to her depressive symptoms, and it is quite likely that she would have responded to electroconvulsive treatments.

On discharge she remained agitated and with a feeling of hopelessness. About three years after discharge, the patient committed suicide by freezing to death. She was found in a city park with a note asking for forgiveness. In retrospect, it seems it would have been wise to treat her with ECT.

The diagnosis would be major depression, unipolar type. Of special interest is the fact that her father had committed suicide probably in a depressive period. Another point of importance is that she was chronically depressed. A follow-up study over a long period of time has indicated that depressions in older people may last for prolonged periods of time but they are not interminable. Thus, a person may be depressed for ten years and when followed 15 years after the admission will have turned out to have been well for five.

Case 2. Mrs F. was a 35-year-old married woman who was admitted because of depression, loss of appetite, complaints of pain in the head, and the belief that her head was filled with either blood or water and should be drained. She had had this illness for about two months and had delivered a baby about four months before admission. Her expression was sad. She described herself as being half asleep and half dead and blamed herself for a variety of things. Her family history was negative, although her father was reported to be nervous. The patient herself had had an attack of depression at the time of her father's death, six years previously. She had not been either treated or hospitalized for this, though it was considered a significant change.

At the time of admission, she stated that she would have jumped into the river if it were not a sin. She remained in the hospital for a period of about 1½ years. For her first 2–3 days, her spirits improved slightly. After 1½ years she was eating better and sleeping well and was able to smile although she felt herself to be still depressed. She had lost her ideas about having fluid in her head. She remained ill for about 3–6 months at home, but on follow-up seven months after her admission she was noted to have a much improved mental condition.

Comment: This is a patient who today would be treated with antidepressant medication or ECT. She was not markedly suicidal though such thoughts had passed through her mind. No doubt the treatment of first choice in most cases would be antidepressant medication. Her first depression occurred following the death of her father. Ordinarily depressions that occur in the period of bereavement are not incapacitating but certainly hers was.

Case 3. Mrs Mc. was a 62-year-old woman admitted because of depression, agitation, and fear of losing her mind. This illness had lasted for one year. She was agitated, paced the floor, and rocked back and forth in a chair, groaning to herself. She had become unkempt and refused to take baths or do her hair. She was unable to take care of her housework and talked of suicide. Her mental status revealed good orientation in memory, and psychometric examination revealed an IQ of 117. In the hospal, she was treated with hydrotherapy and felt better in time. She was in the hospital for a period of about a month and at the end of that time her facial expression had changed to one of calmness and she was neat, pleasant, and engaged in regular activities. Her diagnosis was that of involutional melancholia, which may be defined as a depression occurring for the first time around the time of the menopause.

Comment. Another diagnosis would be of that of major depression or unipolar depression. She had never had a mania. She was considered cured at discharge. No specific treatment had been given and were she to be admitted in modern times she no doubt would have received some specific antidepressant therapy. In follow-up, it is notable that she was considered well nine months after her discharge; but she must have become ill a second time because six years after discharge she was admitted to a state hospital for treatment of her mental state. The episodic nature of the illness is typical of depressive illness. At that point, she was lost to follow-up.

Case 4. Mr E. was a 46-year-old, married man who prior to admission stated that he attempted suicide by placing his head over a gas burner. He became unconscious but soon regained wakefulness. He stated that he had been subject to melancholic spells for years and said that he had planned suicide on numerous occasions. He believed that he was no good, that his wife was wasting her time on him, and that she was wasting money paying for his hospitalization. Thus, he appeared to be a rather chronic patient at the time of admission. He had an air of friendly co-operation and took the whole admission more or less as a joke, much as a patient with gallows humour might do. He had no impairment of intellectual facilities. His mood was considered depressed and hopeless and rather desperate. There were no delusions or hallucinations. As noted above, he had had a whole series of depressions which had occurred off and on for at least four years prior to the admission. The episode for which he was admitted had lasted five or six weeks. He spent about a week in the hospital. Five months after admission he was followed up and was working full time. On follow-up two years later, it was noted that he had had two severe depressions since leaving the hospital.

Comment. It should be noted that this patient did reasonably well although he did have subsequent depressions. Today he would no doubt be put on either antidepressant medication or lithium in an attempt to prevent subsequent episodes. Data exist which indicate that prevention of subsequent episodes is possible with this kind of medication. Should these drugs have been ineffective, a trial of cognitive therapy might be indicated. His diagnosis would be that of major depression, recurrent. Of course, he would be unipolar rather than bipolar in that he had never had a mania.

Case 5. This was a 50-year-old single farmer who in the spring became depressed and was admitted to the hospital several months later, in the winter. He was pleasant and co-operative, but slowed up in his thinking and his movements. He was restless during the day and slept poorly at night. He lost interest in his usual activities and did little work around the farm. He was not interested in socializing which was contrary to his usual self. The patient had suffered two depressions previously, one 31 years before and another four years before. He lacked spontaneity and described himself as feeling sad and lacking interest. He did feel that his eyes looked peculiar but there was no evidence of any other thing that appeared to be anything like hallucinations or delusions. His IQ was 93. His family history was positive in that a brother, age 65, had suffered a depression at the age of 42. The patient was in the hospital for a period of about two months. His diagnosis was manic–depressive, depressed. He never had had a mania.

Halfway through his hospitalization, improvement occurred. He became more interested in other people, mixed well, and was discharged. It was not felt that he was absolutely well, however. A letter from the patient six years later stated, 'I am getting along very well since I was in the hospital in 1938 and 1939. Whatever periods of depressed feelings I have are of short duration. It took me about two years before I felt completely well. I have been working for almost two years now. I don't see why I can't get along all right in the future.'

Comment. This patient improved with non-specific hospital care. It is of interest that he had an episode many years before and then one only four years before admission. As men with depression get older, they are likely to have increasing numbers of episodes. For this reason, the patient would have been a legitimate candidate for some prophylactic therapy with either antidepressants or lithium. No doubt today he would be treated for his acute depression with antidepressants at the time of admission.

Case 6. This is a 47-year-old woman who is married. For three months before admission she had been excited, overactive, overtalkative, and had expansive ideas. She showed bursts of irritability and profanity during admission. She was elated and effusive in her talk, often facetious and domineering. She was admitted in mid-October but had become ill in mid-July. At that time, her talk had become peculiar. She would laugh and sing loudly with untiring effort. She was admitted to a local hospital and then after a few months to the Iowa Psychiatric Hospital. Previously, at 14, she had had a period of depression in which she felt despondent, cried continuously and had trouble thinking. She had to be removed from school. Two years prior to admission, at the age of 45, she had a surgical removal of gall stones and an uterine suspension and resection of an ovary. She had become excited and elated with pressure of speech and flight of ideas. After several days of sedation, she returned to her normal state. These symptoms recurred several months later and again remitted spontaneously in five weeks.

For the present admission she was in the hospital for about eighteen months, made no change with hospital care or hydrotherapy. She left the hospital to enter a private sanatorium for further care. She was discharged from the sanatorium after a short stay. Three months later she committed suicide by shooting herself with her husband's revolver. Until three weeks prior to her death, she did well for ten days and then became depressed.

Comment. This patient was never treated with anything very specific. Today she would be treated with haloperidol or chlorpromazine or some other neuroleptic for her mania. She might have been put on lithium for prophylaxis of subsequent episodes. Perhaps one of the most important things that would be necessary is that she be followed by a concerned physician who kept track of her changing clinical state. Her diagnosis at the time of admission was considered manic–depressive, manic. Of course, she was a bipolar patient. Manias are often followed by severe depressions during which it is very important that the patient be monitored for suicidal intent. In general, the great period of risk for suicide is in the year following discharge from the hospital.

Case 7. This was a 50-year-old, married woman who was admitted in 1931. Her attack manifested itself in excitability, irritability, and antagonistic feelings toward her husband. At the time of admission, she was in a high or euphoric state. She talked voluminously and was very circumstantial. Everything seemed wonderful to her. She was in an exalted mood. Though she had no delusions, she did say that her dead brother appeared to her at dawn each morning and instructed her as to her general conduct. She recovered totally from this episode. Six years later in 1937 the patient was admitted a second time. She was incoherent and talked continuously. She did not seem particularly elated or depressed at that time, but during her stay in the hospital she became euphoric, talked spontaneously, showed overactivity, flight of ideas, incoherent speech, and poor memory and disorientation. She became excited and destructive. Her diagnosis was manic–depressive psychosis, mania. She was unimproved and after a few days was discharged to a state hospital. By three months later, the patient had returned home from the state hospital, had taken full charge of her house and was considered to be well.

Comment. This patient was obviously very difficult to manage. No doubt she would have been treated with one of the major tranquillizers, such as haloperidol, chlorpromazine, or thioridazine. She had six years between episodes and, as a consequence, it is quite likely nobody would put her on lithium for prevention of subsequent episodes in that she might not have another for a long period of time or ever.

Case 8. Mr N. is a 29-year-old married man who was admitted in 1936 to the University of Iowa Psychiatric Hospital. He had been in a state hospital a few years prior to this admission, had spent three months there and was discharged as well. He remained well until three weeks before the hospitalization at the Iowa Psychiatric Hospital. At the time of the admission, he had developed delusions of grandeur, principally that he had a lot of money. He could not sleep, and was overactive and overtalkative. He thought that he had bought out Henry Ford. Another idea that he had was that he would go to Alaska and make a fortune selling electric refrigerators to the Eskimos. His attack four years ago at the state hospital had been quite similar. His mental status showed overtalkativeness, circumstantiality, difficulty sleeping, irritability, delusions of grandeur. At one point, he thought he was President Roosevelt and at another point he thought he owned Ethiopia and had placed his flag there. His mood was euphoric. He was in the hospital for a month and did not improve. He was sent on to a state hospital. His diagnosis was manic–depressive, manic type. He improved sufficiently to leave the state hospital and was lost to follow-up in a few months. However, it was felt that he had not totally recovered.

Comment. This is a patient who probably should have been followed somewhat more closely. His excitement could have been treated in a variety of ways. The fastest way to calm a person down from a mania is with neuroleptic drugs or with ECT. It is possible that he would have been a legitimate candidate for lithium as a prophylaxis for further episodes.

Case 9. Mr W., a married man, was brought to the hospital after a history of a mild depression followed by acute excitement. He was restless, excited, and slept poorly at the time of admission. He was hyperactive and it was difficult to restrain him. There was an overproduction of speech. His associations were superficial. There was a great deal of word play. Hallucinations had been present, both visual and auditory. There were numerous ideas of persecution, and at times the patient seemed to be terror stricken. The mood was euphoric. He had short episodes of crying (microdepressions). He was considered to be confused and somewhat disoriented. This mental state had developed after his mother had died in an apoplectiform seizure, and his son was operated on for removal of carcinoma of the testicle. Of course, these events upset the patient very much and perhaps they had something to do with precipitating the excitement. He remained in the hospital for a period of a month and then was sent on to a state hospital. He left the state hospital after having been hospitalized for a period of ten months. He gradually improved and was considered well at the time of follow-up. He managed his farm capably, renewed associations with his neighbours, re-entered his Masonic lodge and took part in political activities.

Comment. This patient was in two hospitals from June 1935 to March 1936. He was then discharged for a period of five months. Today his hospitalization would be much shorter. He would be actively treated with neuroleptic drugs or lithium for the acute episode. He would not be a subject who would be considered for prophylactic treatment in that he had only one episode. Not having shown multiple episodes up to that time one would consider that he might have a good prognosis without putting him on a prophylactic drug. Another way in which he might have been treated would have been electroconvulsive therapy. Suffice it to say that the modern treatment of such a patient would shorten the amount of necessary hospitalization and care by a good bit in that the person would be actively and effectively treated with more specific kinds of therapy.

Glossary

Alerting responses. Responses to appropriate stimuli, such as turning towards a parent's voice in an infant of more than four months. Alerting responses are impaired or absent in reactive attachment disorder of infancy.

Anaclitic depression. Essentially synonymous with reactive attachment disorder. It is seen in infants separated from their mothers for long periods of time and shows the same symptoms that are noted under reactive attachment disorder.

Atypical depression. A brief episode of depression that is not associated with the full group of symptoms of major depression. Another definition includes seriously disabled patients who do not have classic signs of depression such as early morning awakening and loss of appetite but are chronically unhappy and may even sleep too much rather than too little. A third definition involves an admixture of depressive symptoms with anxiety, phobias, and hysterical features.

Bipolar depression. A depression occurring in a person who has also suffered from a mania some time in the past.

Brief depression. A depression syndrome which is related closely in time and content to some stressful event.

Concordance. Seen in twins. Where both members of the pair have the same illness, they are considered concordant. Should they not have the same illness, they are considered discordant.

Cyclothymic disorder. A chronic disturbance in mood involving many periods of depression and hypomania. These depressions and hypomanias are not of sufficient severity or duration to be considered a major mood disturbance.

Delusions. Fixed false ideas.

Depression spectrum disease. An ordinary depression occurring in a person who has a family history of alcoholism and/or antisocial personality. Usually the family history is that of alcoholism. Such an individual may have a family member with a depression as well but may not have a family member with mania.

Distractibility. Inability to keep one's mind or eyes on a single thing.

Dysthymic disorder. A large extent synonymous with the concept of neurotic depression. There is a chronic depressed mood and some symptoms but these are not of sufficient severity to be considered a major depressive illness. Often there are normal periods between depression, which periods last a few days to a few weeks.

Endogenous-psychotic depression. A depression thought to be due to biological factors which manifests itself by severe depressive symptoms as well as by such symptoms as delusions and hallucinations on occasion. Severity manifests itself by inability to function in a normal social situation and frequently hospitalization is needed.

Familial pure depressive disease. An ordinary depression that occurs in a person who has a family history of depression in another family member. No family member may have mania, alcoholism, or antisocial personality.

Grandiosity. A feeling that one has unusual powers or is descended from an important person.

Hypomania. Mild mania.

Involutional melancholia. A serious depression occurring in an individual during the involutional stage of life (45–60 years). Thus, in women it would occur around the time of the menopause. The onset of illness would be in the involutional stage of development. Currently, most evidence indicates that involutional melancholia should not be considered as a separate mood disorder.

Major depression. An episode characterized by depressive mood and loss of interest or pleasure in usual activities. This depression is prominent, relatively persistent, and associated with such symptoms as appetite disturbance, weight loss, sleep problems, agitation, retardation, decreased energy, feelings of worthlessness or guilt, trouble concentrating, and thoughts of death or suicide or suicide attempts.

Mania. An abnormal state characterized by an unusually high mood, racing thoughts, overtalkativeness, overactivity, distractibility, grandiosity, and financial extravagance.

Medical model. A way of looking at an illness or a syndrome in which the aspects of the illness are broken down into a definition, a clinical picture, a natural history, a cause, and a treatment. It is this way in which physicians look at all medical illnesses.

Micro-depressions. Short episodes of depression of 30 seconds to a couple of minutes which occur in individuals who mainly are suffering from mania.

Neurotic depression. A depression of varying severity, though usually not severe, in an individual who has had a stormy personal life up to the time that he or she became depressed.

Glossary

Placebo. Generally an inert substance which may cause some desirable effects in individuals to whom it is administered. Thus, a sugar pill which was given in place of an antidepressant pill would be considered a placebo.

Primary affective disorder. The opposite of secondary depression. A primary affective disorder is mood disorder that may either be bipolar or unipolar. No other psychiatric illness predates the mania or the depression. Therefore, the mania or depression is considered primary.

Prolonged depression. Depression developing in association with prolonged exposure to a stressful situation.

Psychogenic depressive psychosis. *See* Reactive depressive psychosis.

Reactive attachment disorder. Seen in infancy and is manifested by lack of appropriate responsiveness and an apathetic mood. Physiologically there is a failure to thrive, manifesting itself by poor physical development.

Reactive depression. A depression of mild to moderate severity, usually not severe that is a response to a difficult life stress.

Reactive depressive psychosis (synonym: psychogenic depressive psychosis). Serious depression or excitement associated with difficult life events and manifested by depressive symptoms as well as delusions and hallucinations.

Retardation. A slowing down of speech or movement.

Schizophrenia. A chronic illness manifesting itself by delusions, hallucinations, a blunting of feeling or inappropriate response to ordinary stimuli. Other symptoms are ideas that are expressed incoherently and marked withdrawal from ordinary social events.

Secondary depression. An ordinary depression which occurs in context of another psychiatric illness, such as anxiety neurosis, alcoholism, schizophrenia, etc. This depression appears similar to primary depression but occurs after onset of another illness. There is some reason to believe that secondary depressions also occur in the context of a serious medical illness.

Sporadic depressive disease. An ordinary depression in an individual who has a negative family history for alcoholism, antisocial personality, depression, or mania.

Subjective agitation. A feeling on the part of an individual that he is shaky or nervous inside and cannot sit still. This does not necessarily have to manifest itself to an observer.

Unipolar depression. A depression which occurs in the absence of any history of mania. Unipolar depression may occur as a single episode or may manifest itself by multiple episodes of depression.

Index